The Alchemy of Modern Medicine

A Naturopath's Memoirs during Breast Cancer and Reconstruction

Dr. Lynn Mikel

Many thanks to all my dear friends of whom there are too many to mention by name but who are part of my story!

A special thank-you to my family who have been there for me through so much.

Mom for her wisdom and for teaching me by example to reach for my dreams and to ask, "If not now, when?!"

Dad for his love, affection, admiration, and belief in me and my choices!

Thanks to my three brothers for their presence in my life and commitment to our family and their own.

Sue for her tenderness and ALWAYS showing up for me!

Judy for her strength and resilience and for the time she's taken to create our bond! What a wonderful "sisterhood" we have created together!

Joseph for the beautiful art work creating the cover. I am humbled and inspired by your creativity.

Marie for the final editing support to get this to completion! How nice to have you still in my life.

Gary for your love and your faith that "All is well" and reminding me over and over again of both! Also, thanks for your humor and seeing the beauty in me always.

And thank you, Christy, for her patience, honesty, and that Spirit I so admire. We've gone through a lot of life together so far, and my wish is we enjoy much more!

Preface

To whom am I writing? Why am I writing this memoir? These questions were posed to me by my writing mentor, and I pondered the answers. Initially, I was writing for myself, maybe so I wouldn't forget the story, emotions, drama, and steps of evolution in my process of facing cancer. It was also a testament to my faith as I really believed there was a Higher Power I could surrender to that would transform this episode of my life into something meaningful.

I had grown through a number of physical and emotional challenges earlier in my life by finding a spirituality that seemed to help. I had decided that God was love. I also decided that love was letting go of fear. My spiritual journey was to practice the Presence of God in all situations of my life, which meant opening to the possibility of good outcomes despite appearances.

Miracles and healing had happened for me in the past, and I wanted to record this opportunity hoping that would happen again.

My writing mentor said it seemed I was trying to find meaning. Yes, it felt important to bring something out of this that could be transformative, not only for me, but perhaps for others.

My reservation about writing was the time it would take. I knew the surgery and healing would go on for 6 months to a year and would involve a lot of time focused on appointments, surgery, and my self-care. I felt very conflicted about taking additional time for this writing process. Medical school had taken seven long years, and I still felt guilt about the sacrifice in time not given to my daughter, Christy, who was 9 years old when I graduated. The writing seemed selfish if I was taking more time away from her, but there was such a strong message within to write that I could not deny it. It felt like an assignment!

Looking back now that I have survived and with a beautiful outcome, there is definitely a reason to share my story. At least once a week, a patient walking through my door, or someone calling my office will ask for information about breast cancer and recovery. The information I have to share is important for anyone looking for alternative and complementary approaches to breast health. My personal story is about healing physically, emotionally and spiritually through this challenge. It became another opportunity for me to awaken to a new way of being more whole in myself, and it emerged in the process of finding my way back to health and balance. Surrender was not about giving up but about letting go and seeing what happened. As I learned to love myself and allow myself to be cared for, I had to confront all the hurts within me that have kept those two things at a distance. Giving those places of hurt some voice, attention, and compassion led me to wake up deep parts of myself and later to feel more trust, self-acceptance, inner freedom, and peace. Hopefully, sharing this part of my path will inspire women with their own health challenges to be emotionally and spiritually open in their process so they can also find a way to respond with grace and openness to receive lessons and blessings that are waiting to be received!

When I was first diagnosed with breast cancer I called Dr. Bill Mitchell, a good friend and mentor at Seattle Naturopathic College, Bastyr University, to talk through my protocols I was following. I wanted his confirmation I was doing the right things and to receive any additional input he might add to my efforts to stay well and survive this. Months later, we talked, and I told him of my wonderful outcome and that I had written my story. He was adamant that this be published. He said I must get the information out to the public! "This is too important not to share," he said. Dr. Mitchell passed away less than a year later in February of 2007, with my writing sitting on a shelf. My shock and grief at his death immediately took me to those last words he said to me with his encouragement and all the genuine passion he felt for our medicine. I dedicate this to his love and support, personally and professionally. It is with humility and courage that I offer this personal account of my inner and outer journey so that others may also find the alchemy of grace to transform them through whatever form of treatment they undertake. It is possible to heal!

Chapter 1

To Practice the Presence of God

... Even in this? My mantra the past 20 years had been to practice the Presence of God in my life. That meant to expect a miracle, know that God is good beyond appearances, have faith that all is well, and expect outcomes for my highest good. But how, sitting in the waiting room for a biopsy on suspected breast cancer, was I to do that? I had gone in for my scheduled mammogram without anxiety or concern certain it would be another routine screening checked off my to-do list. They had quite a time getting my small breasts squished into their machine and seemed to take so many views. I became concerned about all the radiation exposure. I had waited over six years to do this exam because for the last two mammograms they also took way too many x-rays.

Apparently, my right breast had some sort of area difficult to view each time I did this! It had always turned out okay when they finally got the view but took half a dozen views to get there, and we were doing this all over again! However, on this day it was the left breast that had a couple suspicious areas. I was sent back to the waiting room with fears starting to rise as I waited for results. They wanted me to stay for an immediate ultrasound view and biopsy if needed. As I waited for that, all my positive thoughts in the world were overshadowed by fear, dread, and memories of grief. I had lost my husband to cancer eight years earlier. I felt so alone in that cold place. Where did all my faith go in those moments? And it just got worse.... The technician did the biopsy efficiently, but from her concerned manner, I knew there was strong suspicion this was cancer. Her response was poised and appropriate in not diagnosing but left me with the conclusion that, from her experience and judgment, the result would be positive. "Positive" seemed such a contradictory term to use...positive for breast cancer. They rushed me over to the scheduling area for an appointment with the surgeon "as soon as possible", leaving me little doubt as to the suspicion. I sat with a kind nurse assisting in the biopsy, and, when it was over, tears finally began streaming down my face. As she held the dressing with pressure over my breast she listened to me weep and to my desperate plea to God that this not happen to me. I wondered how I could go through this after what I experienced with Chuck and his death from cancer. He died a slow, painful death over two years to metastatic lung cancer. The horror of watching his decline and the deep grief even seven years later still felt acute. It seemed too much for me to suffer. Eventually, my life did go on after his death ... I graduated from medical school, and I had found a new partner. I was gradually reinvesting in life and love only to have this demon appear AGAIN to threaten all that I held dear.

One of the first things I did the next day was call the Silent Unity prayer line where someone would anonymously pray for your requests. The woman on the phone was a little short with me because I wanted more than one request. I requested prayers for me and also for my daughter Christy and partner Gary. I did not want either of them to have to go through this cancer ordeal; I knew first hand it would be tough. Christy was five years old when her father died. She knew he had cancer, watched his bones break, and his multiple surgeries. She experienced him occasionally losing his vitality and patience from being in excruciating pain. She watched me fall apart over and over as we repeatedly got disappointing news as the cancer kept spreading. She was even playing in his hospital bed those last days before his body finally gave out, wasted away to nothing and him hardly recognizing who we were. "Please not this again, for her sake," I cried and prayed. Gary was a Viet Nam veteran, child of an abusive father, and still emotionally recovering from a rough divorce. He, too, had experienced enough traumas in his life. "Please, not this for him either," I cried and prayed. The woman on the phone was generous in finding a way to include all of them in her prayers. The first thing she prayed for was that I would have good and skilled caregivers I could trust.... The rest I don't really remember. I just remember thinking; "Caregivers. But I don't want to have caregivers. I don't want to have cancer"! It planted a seed that began to take root. The few days expected for the biopsy results turned into over a week. The waiting seemed so long. I was at my office the day I received the biopsy results. I was back to work but definitely distracted during the waiting and began to have doubts about what I had to offer my patients if I couldn't even keep myself well! I got the call with the diagnosis. "You have noninvasive ductal carcinoma insitu (DCIS)." The woman was professional and appropriate, however, unable to give me any further information except to tell me my surgeon would discuss the treatment recommendations and options. I felt relieved finally to know what we were dealing with; disappointed it was positive for cancer; but knowing it was the very best prognosis with that type of cancer, DCIS. I was unclear yet about treatment options, and my very worst fear was to lose my breast.

My heart was pounding, and I looked around the quiet, peaceful space of my office and realized I had to be still. I lit a candle, sat in my chair and tried to still my mind and the heart that were reeling. I knew I had to hold on to my light of faith and hope. I had done my best at this in regards to many other challenges in the past and found it really helped me face my fears and realize better outcomes

11

than I could have imagined. Faith and hope brought me through Christy's birth, seven years of medical school, through my experience with Chuck's illness and death, and through the daily process of practicing as a doctor all with more success than I thought possible. Over and Over I had become willing to surrender my fears to my higher power or God's love …amazed life worked out when I prayed for grace to participate the best I could and let go. Letting go of control and opening up to the days that would follow was not a new practice for me but still not easy. However, I knew my attitude and trust were so important if my outcome with this diagnosis was going to turn out positive. Those minutes of surrender were lonely and surreal, yet they brought some strength to move into the next step of facing what I ultimately had to face. I called Gary and relayed the diagnosis. He coincidentally had talked with a buddy at work whose wife had gone through the same type of diagnosis. His friend had learned a lot about DCIS and knew it was, in effect, precancerous. His wife had been treated successfully with a lumpectomy, recovered without much trouble, and had no recurrence in nearly five years. I felt thankful Gary had some information and was not freaked out. However, it also seemed he was taking it a little too casually. I knew the treatment would involve multiple doctor appointments and likely involve some surgery with the possibility of radiation. I felt my resistance to the time, stress, and medicine that we would be brought into and knew it would not be easy. He had no idea.

During this initial shock of getting the diagnosis, I was aware of a whole slew of memories coming back to me. I relived the way Chuck had been told he had cancer. No one wanted to be the one to relay the "bad news" so a technician was given the task instead of his primary care physician. "Of course you have cancer," the technician told us, seemingly annoyed because it had been left up to him to tell us. I was still so angry at the way they wrote him off from the beginning with his diagnosis of metastatic lung cancer. They gave him about 6 months to live. When I asked about support groups, they said most lung cancer patients don't live long enough to benefit from the groups, so don't bother. Of course, it was not a good diagnosis, but he was in good shape, in a happy marriage, and with a new baby. Christy was three years old when he was diagnosed. He had everything to live for. Didn't that count in his favor for something? I found a support group for him, and the 6 months turned into over two years. A year and a half of that time was quality time with us. We took a trip to Europe, took an Alaskan cruise, and, most importantly, he had time with his little girl who needed all the time he could share with her. I was still furious when I remembered the radiologist he worked with. On our initial consultation, just getting the diagnosis, she read over his chart and laid out the treatment plan. Then, she glibly added, "Well, I guess you don't have to worry about sunscreen anymore". He had melanoma in the past, and I guess she was saying... "You're going die anyway"! It felt like a death sentence, and I will never forgive her for planting those seeds of demise in his heart. My heartache and anger, always just beneath the surface, were reawakened. More memories surfaced; bringing him to radiation every other day for weeks, assisting him to and from the car from his wheel chair, watching him withdraw in pain, helping him onto the x-ray table as gently as we could, and sitting in the waiting room with others who were dying.

Despite and because of the flood of memories, I knew this situation I was facing could be a potential opportunity to heal my anger at the medical system. I remembered my Unity chaplain's prayer for good "caregivers" and knew it was an opportunity to have a different experience with them than Chuck and I had. I felt deep in my being that I would have good people around me and that there could be an aspect of care that had been missing for Chuck. I knew that this would happen only to the degree that I could be open to the possibility and surrender my anger. It would definitely be a challenge, but the stakes were high enough now, and I was motivated and relieved to finally do so.

Gary was an angel going with me to my next appointments. It was so different to have someone there beside me, unlike the biopsy procedure where I felt so alone. Gary's physical support was so comforting. My first visit to the surgeon was what I expected, technically. She described the DCIS as precancerous yet advanced enough to warrant surgery. I was told sixty percent of patients with DCIS go on to experience metastatic cancer if not treated. She briefly described a lumpectomy the recovery, and expected outcome. With tears welling up in my eyes, I told her this was hitting me hard and a little about my experience with my husband's cancer and death hoping she would have some insight to my fears and emotions. She listened quietly and made no comment. Her manner was cool and professional. She gave me very little of her emotional self. I wondered if she was depressed or just worn out from dealing with cancer every day. Who was this woman I was entrusting with my care? Not surprised yet still disappointed I didn't get the compassionate response or rapport with her that I would have liked; I tried to trust that she was the best at her skill as the surgeon.

Gary was hit a little harder after that first meeting, with the medical language and stoic environment. He took the information in with more seriousness. The interaction with the medical system was hanging over us like a bad mood. Surgery was scheduled a week later, and the waiting this time went rather quickly. During that week, I talked with Gary's friend's wife, and she described her experience with breast cancer in retrospect as a "bump in the road". She recovered fairly easily, physically and emotionally. I got a second opinion about my treatment plan via her referral. This doctor was not quite so sure a lumpectomy was the best choice as there was a suspicious second calcification that had not been biopsied. It was his opinion to do another biopsy, and, if that was also DCIS, he would recommend a mastectomy. I came away feeling I had made the right choice to want the least invasive procedure. I did call my doctor and asked her if she planned to take the other calcification out as well. She assured me that was her plan and that the lumpectomy was still her recommendation.

"All is well" was Gary's mantra to me, and it really helped when he would whisper it in my ear. I began to hear that in my head and was visualizing the cancer cells gone. Two days after I received that phone call with the cancer diagnosis, a new friend asked me if I would like to attend a "healing mass." A priest who had been given the gift of healing was performing a charismatic healing mass that Thursday night. My Old Catholic background was my fallback in times of crisis. During Chuck's dying process, there had been many times when I would visit the campus chapel at Bastyr University where I was studying Naturopathic Medicine. I would go and sit at the feet of the statue of Mary and say prayers, rosaries, and pleas for more time with him. She had always given me comfort and strength to meet that day. I was sure she brought the Goddess of Wisdom available to me for those many challenging tests through the six year long doctorial program. Despite all the ideology conflicts I had with the

Catholic Church, underneath, it still provided a foundation for my belief in a Supreme Power of love guiding my life. I never doubted there was a God, and I believe that came from my Catholic upbringing and even my Catholic ancestry.

The Healing Mass service was comforting though kind of funny trying to get a group of suburban-type Catholics to be charismatic. The end of the mass was a real stretch for most of us. We each stood at the altar while the Priest did the sacrament of anointing the sick. There were people behind us to catch us because sometimes when people received the Holy Spirit, they fell over. The people behind encouraged us to be open and receptive to whatever experience we had. They reassured us that even if we didn't fall over, we still could receive the Holy Spirit; it was different for everyone. As I stood in line waiting my turn, I began to feel a powerful energy around me. My legs felt weak, and I wondered if it was because I was so scared for myself, hungry, or maybe some healing was really available for me to experience. The priest approached me, and instantaneously I was in an altered state. My eyes closed, and he felt very close to my head while he was talking in Latin. There was the aroma of incense, and I heard people speaking in tongues up, down, and all around me. My legs began to tremble, then, a voice encouraged me to let go. I fell back into someone's arms and onto the floor. I was surrounded in light, felt warm, stunned, and acutely alive. After that sacrament of anointing, my sense of well-being improved quite dramatically. I felt a new physical energy that continued from that day forward.

Emotionally, this was a time of wrestling with feelings of guilt. Perhaps that fallback feeling was one of the negative influences from being raised Catholic. I felt the cancer somehow must have been my fault. Perhaps I hadn't followed a healthy enough diet, hadn't exercised enough, or hadn't paid enough attention to my emotions. I felt that if any of those things were true, then my credibility as a doctor was gone. If I hadn't kept myself well, how could I advise others? I obsessed as to whether or not I had some toxic exposure and what if it had also affected Christy. My worry, anxiety, guilt, shame, and sadness were so automatic. I knew they were some of the familiar negative self-talk that I had struggled with my whole life. After 25 years of Jungian dream work and therapy, I knew that these feelings came from the hurts and wounded places in my psyche. I did everything in my power to listen to a rational, loving, and compassionate voice either from me or from others as I dug myself out of that hole of self-deprecation. I tried to use positive tools to turn down those negative thoughts and feelings. I believed my thoughts created my reality and that my thoughts were responsible for my feelings. Somehow I had to use the tools I'd learned to honor my feelings but also practice new thoughts that could ultimately change my emotions and help shape the experience I wanted... health and wholeness!

One of my favorite tools, and a very powerful tool of survival I had learned, was to create a "treasure map" or collage of what I wanted. So, I created a collage visualizing my breasts healthy and beautiful. I pictured a woman powerful, celebrating, happy, and whole! My treasure maps had always created a positive result for achieving goals, and I used them when I was inspired to create an outcome. I had used them for having a girl when I was pregnant; getting accepted for medical school; graduating from Bastyr; becoming a doctor; and even for Gary and the life we had together. They worked by empowering the subconscious cooperation with achieving conscious goals. Additionally, I used affirmations and visualized healthy breasts. I used EFT, a technique to change subconscious patterns through affirmation and acupressure. I went to a Chinese doctor and got Chinese herbs to boost my immune system. I consulted with another Naturopath to go over the details of the naturopathic protocols for cancer protection and surgery. I got his professional input on radiation and tamoxafin. I researched support groups and talked to a woman from Angel Care, a support for women with breast cancer.

Despite the feeling of frantic desperation at times, the concrete steps I took doing the treasure map, my supplements, exercise, Chinese and herbal medicines, spiritual contacts, and use of psycho/spiritual tools that I had used before ... there was hope and relief that I could influence a positive outcome. Surrendering was not giving up but letting go. By taking some action, it was then possible for me to go forward practicing the Presence of God in each moment, expecting my prayers to be answered, and that everything would be okay. I also knew I didn't always get what I wanted but usually what I needed. That meant there could be a lot to accept, but it could still turn out to be a blessing!

Chapter 2

Surgery was a Scary Day

I didn't sleep well the night before surgery, anxious about the result and how I would look. Would my breast have some big chunk taken out of it? The surgeon hadn't really described any details of my surgery so I had no idea what to expect. The consultation prior to surgery was mostly about the recommended protocol, in this case the lumpectomy. I had asked questions, but they were answered more in regards to the statistics supporting this procedure. It wasn't until the follow-up visit after the surgery that she explained a little about the technique and expected outcome. It seemed that there had been such a "rush" to get in there and begin the treatment. We got to the hospital at 5:30 a.m. and sat in the waiting room for an hour and a half. Was the early hour just to be sure we made it to surgery? It certainly didn't make it easier for us! Finally, we were brought back to the pre-surgery area where I was asked to put on the usual hospital garb, a very thin gown with socks. I was taken to an area with a dozen other people where we each were put into a curtain-partitioned cubicle. About an hour later, an anesthesiologist introduced himself. He asked if I was allergic to anything, wrote that down, then leaving, said we would talk more a little later. That never happened. A nurse came thirty minutes later and put in an IV. She gave us some information about recovery and use of the pain medication following the procedure. Eventually, they brought me in a wheelchair to the same area where the original biopsy and mammogram /ultrasound had been done. There, I waited about a half an hour in a storage room that was also used as a backup treatment room. I was incredibly cold, really alone, and I felt like I'd been put in a closet! Finally, I was retrieved from there, and they started the challenging process of getting mammogram pictures of my breast to place identifying needles to show the surgeon areas to be excised. As my breasts were small and the areas were deep, they were basically trying to squeeze my chest in a machine that allowed no room for my head to be perpendicular with my body. Imagine pushing your chest into a doorway with a security chain, then trying to close the door while inserting 6-inch needles about a dozen times because you can't get the door closed! The intense pain didn't bother me as much as the excessive amount of radiation my breast was getting. Naturopaths tend to be cautious about cancer promoters like pesticides and hormones. These chemicals can mimic estrogen and encourage cells to grow (including hormone sensitive cancer cells). Radiation also has damaging effects to DNA that potentially mutate cells to become cancer cells. I questioned the multiple exposures during the mammogram, but my concerns were always discounted. I also had concerns about a needle biopsy pulling cancer cells through clean tissue and possibly potentiating the spread of the dangerous cells. This too was discounted. The technician said she had never heard of this before and was adamant the surgeon required this. I had just read an article in a medical journal the week before that biopsies were potentially dangerous and that surgical excision was a much safer option. We had gotten to that point anyway!

Finally, after a dozen x-rays with a few useable films and with needles in place to identify the areas for excision, I was wheeled back for surgery. My little gown was not adequate in keeping me warm in that cold room. The assistant offered me a light cotton blanket, but it did little to warm me. By the time they were getting me to surgery, I was trembling from the cold and nerves. Finally, in surgery, there was my surgeon in a pretty colorful hair net.

She had a completely different disposition. She was smiling and pleasant. I told her I had been visualizing the cancer gone, and she assured me in a few hours that it would be. They laid me out on a very narrow table, just wide enough for my body. Somebody slapped something cold over my legs, and I started trembling even harder. The anesthesiologist pulled my right arm out at 90 degrees. The surgeon pulled my left arm out at 90 degrees to place it out of the way for surgery. The last thing I remember thinking was ...this felt a lot like a crucifixion.

I woke in recovery. The first thing I did was look down at my breast, and, to my huge relief, it was whole and intact. My mantra had been to visualize my "perky little breast, beautiful and intact!" I was so relieved it looked just fine. Though the bandage may be hiding a hole, it seemed pretty much the same. Within a few minutes, Gary was smiling down at me. Bless his heart. He had walked every step of the way with me except to be in the room for the mammogram and surgery. His humor, adoration, and unending love lifted me up through moments of waiting and wondering. I started to cry as tears of relief, grief, gratitude, and built-up anxiety were finally able to be let go. Gary's dear sister JoAnne arrived next, and I couldn't believe that with all she had going on in her life, she would be there for us! She was Gary's angel with her presence and prayers of support.

Days of recovery and waiting for the pathology report followed to confirm the surgery had been a success. Finally, after more than a week, I got another call while I was alone at work. Four of six margins were still involved with the abnormal cells; I would need to follow up with the surgeon. Devastating! Devastating!!! I knew immediately what this meant, and I couldn't believe it. They had not gotten all the cancer. How could this be happening to me? I met with my sisters for dinner that night and somehow kept myself together ... rational, trying to piece together the report, what it meant, still in denial or shock. However, the emotions underneath must have been building up. When I got home with Gary and Christy, I came unglued. Christy, 13 years old, brushed me off when I greeted her with a hug, and that moment undid me. I screamed at her for being so cold and uncaring to her mother who was going through cancer. I stormed off to my room and proceeded to sob for 4 hours. Everything I believed in seemed to be falling away from me and leaving me in a void of fear and loneliness. I knew I was going to lose my breast, and it seemed my worst fear was being realized. Thank God Gary was able to be present in my darkest hour. He held me while my sobbing was interrupted by ranting. Deep, deep pain was surfacing from past, future, and present. So many tears. Where did they all come from? Each one represented a piece of my heart broken day by day, minute by minute as I had lost my first husband Chuck. More tears were for the fear or doubts I had in my ability to be a good mother and doctor. Others tears were for the deep love I had again found with Gary and the fears I could also lose him. Then more tears for myself, that I would be subjected to this barbaric treatment of cutting off my breast. The cathartic evening turned into a sad night and eventually another day. Gary told me a story when we met about how he had gotten through his sad and heartbreaking divorce. He said he just learned to get up every morning and put his pants on.... and somehow he survived. For a couple weeks, that is what it amounted to. I went to work, did research on breast reconstruction, met with plastic surgeons, and worried about outcomes, decisions, metastasis, protocols, and alternatives.

I felt like there was a film of bubble wrap around me. I was in the world but not of it. I would be in the store or post office and hear this voice screaming inside of me "I HAVE BREAST CANCER." How could the world be going on as normal with all this happening inside me?

Chapter 3

I Took the Kind Path and Got Cut Up

Four excruciatingly long weeks of waiting, and preparation for another surgery finally arrived. At first, four weeks seemed like it would be too long to wait, and I could imagine worrying myself sick. However, the time of waiting actually was perfect to the very last day. Once I decided just to show up, grace unfolded and allowed me to return to work with my same commitment and attention I had prior to the whole cancer diagnosis. I was eating healthy with attention to eating more often and avoiding refined sugar. I enjoyed fruits but omitted fruit juice and drank green tea throughout the day. My supplement regimen was extensive. I updated it to include products from cruciferous vegetables that protected me from estrogenic chemicals by assisting their detoxification in the liver. Chinese herbs were incorporated along with daily walks in the evening. I enjoyed these walks, the deep breathing and time in our beautiful neighborhood surrounded by Puget Sound, the trees, the birds, my dog Cubbsy, and wonderful partner Gary. I took a weekend trip with my two sisters to Leavenworth, a Bavarian town in the foothills of the Cascade Mountains. We went on a beautiful hike and created our own little prayer ceremony out in nature. We sat amongst the rocks, plants, and animals in a small circle, closed our eyes, and opened our hearts. Our intention was to evoke empowerment for each of us to find our own "emancipation" in whatever area of life we needed most. I told my sisters to watch the animals that appeared on the walk as animals often have a gift and message when they appear. Amazingly, while taking pictures by a waterfall, a colorful butterfly circled around me then landed on my right breast. Quickly, I was surrounded by three or four more. Later, I learned from my sisters that they had been humoring me about the animal thing, even the healing circle, but it turned out to be a little miracle of Spirit when what we honored was called forth. For me, the butterfly became a symbol of lightening up and letting go. A couple weeks later, Christy had a swim meet in Eastern Washington for a weekend, so we were off on a getaway with two teen girls into makeup, hair, boys and swimming... and in that order. I was amazed, appreciative, and humbled that somehow, through grace again, I was free of worry and fret. I was enjoying my family, the beautiful drive, scenery, the ripe fruit, and, most of all, the peace I felt inside.

Two days before surgery, I was working with a female client and decided to tell her about my condition. When she heard my diagnosis, she immediately contacted a friend, who was also a healer, to see me. She and her friend were both from Poland. She told me people were coming from Canada and even Europe to work with him. He was only 20 minutes away, and I was open to seeing him. He returned my call, and I went that afternoon, wondering if I would even tell Gary because I knew Gary would be very skeptical. I had challenged him in the past about why he was so skeptical in regards to energy healing. I wondered how he could put more faith in allopathic medicine when allopathic interventions were one of the leading causes of death in the U.S.? Anyway, it was my journey, and it felt right to me that afternoon. When I arrived at this man's home, I found a retreat-like setting hidden in the city. He was a compelling figure with a proud stance, deep rich voice and eyes. I asked him as we strolled through his garden, how he came to have this gift. He told me he was born knowing he was special and could use his gift. He told me we all are special and have gifts but usually don't believe. He led me into a small building adjacent to his home that he had built for his healing work and devotion to his faith. The pictures, symbols, and incense spoke to me through the archetypal symbols of the divine. His table was in the center of the room that was built in the shape of a pyramid. As I lay down and looked up, there was a window built in the center of the pyramid that allowed light and elements of nature to illuminate me. I felt I was in the presence of a holy man and was humbled by the opportunity for him to work with me. He spent a few minutes listening to my story and another twenty minutes assessing, then sending and balancing energy. When finished, he told me I was well and my breast was fine. He said I had no need for surgery. He told me it was my time to come to the realization of my oneness with God and accept my purpose of bringing that into expression. He used words I had used myself. He told me that to be well, I must believe this. He also told me my heart chakra was very large, that of a healer, but I was having a little trouble with integration between the right and left sides of my body and in allowing energy to circulate freely throughout my body. He told me I had gifts of healing to share and had this breast cancer experience to be brought to him so as to bring my spiritual awareness to the next level. This contact with him would bring me even more ability to share energy through my hands. Could I believe all this? He expressed the desires of my heart, but still, could I believe? My spiritual lessons in learning to love and forgive myself seemed the gift to share with others. Could I believe my faith could help others? Intuitively, I knew there was truth in his words and had finally found someone who could voice it for me!

What to do? Driving away, I could feel the debate start and wondered how I could decide not to do surgery. "Know the truth, and the truth will set you free." Could I trust that to be enough? I went home and discussed it with

Gary. "If I don't do surgery, would you support me?" I asked. He said, "You know how I feel about "healers." I think you should do surgery, but it is up to you." Christy was adamant she thought surgery was the thing to do, and she didn't want to discuss any alternatives. I called important women in my life and each empowered me in my decision either way. I was thrilled to find they would support me not doing surgery, and I could feel our faith strengthened even by having the discussion. A deeper knowing grew in me that faith was the way to find health and that through faith all things are possible. My growing sisterhood of spiritually committed women was providing me with more and more support. We were all getting stronger through my struggle, and my "problem" began no longer to feel like a burden but an opportunity to bond and strengthen through the feminine aspect of God: empathy, compassion, emotional holding, and touch. A turning point in my dilemma about whether or not to do the mastectomy was a conversation with my Chinese medicine doctor. It was only my second visit with her, and I was amazed at how comfortable I felt in opening up to her. She had this structured, earthy way of wanting to control things. This seemed to put me off at first, but I must have sensed she could let me fall apart because of this very quality in her nature. Her empathy and listening were acute for the details of my life that I had to share. On this second visit, she asked how I was doing. I said. "How do I look?" She said, "Like the cat that just ate the canary." Surprised at her intuition, I laughed and relayed the experience with the healer and what he had said. I asked her if she would support me not doing surgery, and she said, in her opinion, a mastectomy was the best thing to do considering the stage of cancer, where the cancer was found, and the result of the lumpectomy. I took that with disappointment because I wanted to believe my spiritual path, alternative healing arts and love would be enough! Then I let another voice express one reservation to this empathic doctor. If I chose not to do surgery, and the cancer progressed or recurred, would I ever forgive myself the suffering this would cause my daughter Christy? Also, I had struggled my whole life with trying to be perfect and with obsessive-compulsive behavior. Would this need to be spiritual enough not to get cancer and to do everything perfectly haunt me the rest of my life? This healer, in her wise woman persona, listened to me voice my inner dilemma. Finally, she expressed the words that made the difference: "Perhaps the *gentlest* thing you can do for yourself would be to use all the supports available including surgery. No matter what choice you make, you will pursue your spiritual path and alternative healing with passion. Use the surgery as a way to make it a little easier on yourself. My response was a flippant "yeah, gentle, cutting myself up." What a crossroad in my life. I had a realization that to keep my breast but then struggle with perfectionism, self-

43

criticism, doubt, and shame would be more painful than cutting my breast off. It became clear that surgery, risking my life, and deforming my body were very much the gentler, kinder way for me. I was healed in this process in a way that only true healing happens. It was a quantum leap experience in consciousness where the emotional is transmuted to a spiritual awareness, and there is a change in behavior coming from a truly new state of being. I made a difficult choice out of love and compassion for myself.

As the qualities of love and compassion in me were acknowledged and compassionately accepted by this woman and doctor, the act of cutting my breast off symbolized my redemption. It didn't matter if I lost my breast. Some deep place in myself had come back to life...I felt whole, and, yes, I could believe "All is well".

Chapter 4

Initiation to the Amazon

While recovering from the mastectomy, I watched a TV show on "cleavage." It was all about breasts and what they mean in various cultures and contexts. The ancient Greeks had a term for women who cut off one of their breasts to become warriors. They were called Amazons. Sitting on the couch, looking down at my missing breast and wondering about why it all happened, there was an inner surge of power that went through me as I took this in, symbolically. My path of emotional and spiritual growth had been taken to the next level. As much as I disliked the term "fight with cancer", the warrior spirit in me was certainly empowered through this particular experience. In the past few weeks, I had come to feel in the depth of my being that this disease was not the result of something I had done wrong, but, indeed, a reflection of how the earth was suffering. The female breast with its rich supply of fat cells and estrogen was a sponge for all the pollutant chemicals ravaging the earth. It impressed me that the left breast, most commonly affected by breast cancer, was also so close to the heart. The cells of my breast had to have been affected by how my heart ached frequently with emotional distress for the state of our world physically, socially, and politically. Each time my heart grieved about what I read, heard, or experienced, it seemed the cells surrounding my heart had to have been affected! The empowerment I felt with the image of an Amazon was that my feminine empathy must now be turned into constructive power and action! In some way, I had to make a positive contribution to the solution to these problems that distressed me. I asked myself these questions: Was I a warrior? Would my strength and vitality ever return enough to pursue that path? Would I have enough faith and guidance to know how to make a difference?

Awakening from the mastectomy surgery, I remember the anesthesiologist raving about how excellently my surgeons had done their job. It had been a difficult surgery. I had opted to begin the reconstruction at the same time as the mastectomy. That meant that after the breast tissue was excised, the surgeon would place something called an "expander" under the muscle. This was used over the course of 6-8 months to expand the skin gradually to accommodate an implant. Every few weeks, I would be required to go back and have saline injected into the expander to continue the process of expanding and growing the skin. Once that process was complete, another surgery would require replacing the expander with a permanent implant. The surgeon warned me this would be the painful way to go but would eliminate one surgery

47

by combining the mastectomy with the expander placement.

The first memory after waking from the mastectomy surgery was of my husband, Gary, next to me. Tears involuntarily flowed and he reminded me that the first thing I said was to ask him if he still loved me. My self identity was literally in a state of transformation. Despite that doubt, I was blessed with a feeling of security knowing he would be there to watch over me through the next steps in my recovery. Once I was in my hospital room, the awareness of my mother and father's presence was also reassuring until the pain became overwhelming and seemed to spiral out of control. I was really hungry since I hadn't eaten for over 24 hours, but I was so drugged and weak that I could barely sip apple juice. An hour later, I began crying from pain and then started vomiting. My dad left when the crying began, unable to bear seeing his daughter suffer in pain, but he returned later with a beautiful bouquet of flowers from Pike Place Market. I believed that flowers kept the bad spirits away, and I loved him for that gesture of support because as the night progressed, I became very vulnerable to those bad spirits! I was given another pain-killer without effect, then anti-nausea medicine that only worsened the vomiting. In fact, I could feel myself slipping away. I kept reaching for the oxygen tube feeling that if I didn't concentrate enough, my breathing would stop. It got worse, and I could hardly control my mouth to speak my concerns. With great effort, I asked my sisters to call the nurse. In a drugged stupor, I told her I was feeling very anxious like I was going to pass out or stop breathing. As she was injecting another drug, I was telling her that the last time she did that it got worse... but too late? For the next eight hours, I was unconscious, and, according to my sisters and mother, all hell broke loose in that room. My mother and sisters were my guardians, and those praying for me were working overtime! Later, my mother told me she had said, "This hospital better watch out because there are three Amazons in this room!" My sisters and mother insisted to the nurse that a doctor be informed about my condition and that more action be taken. My family was concerned that I was not conscious and not breathing easily. Finally, an attentive and caring nurse seriously responded. He confided to my family that, indeed, everyone was very concerned and my vitals were monitored every ten minutes till they were stable and I had regained consciousness. The next thing I remembered was waking in the middle of the night with Gary by my side and with the pressure of a thousand pounds sitting on my chest. It hurt incredibly to breathe and to move in any way, but I was not nauseous and was fairly clear-headed. The nurse arrived to start a new oral pain medication. Every four hours, we increased the dose so the pain was tolerable as long as I didn't move. Gary, exhausted, finally was trying to sleep in a chair beside my bed, and I asked the nurse if she had a recliner he could use. It helped but was a long night for both of us.

At 5:30 am, a doctor came in leading a group of six residents to my bedside. He said I looked great and could go home. I told him I had had a rough night with a bad reaction to the morphine. He told me I was not on morphine but some other drug. I knew morphine was the first drug they told me I had gotten. He asked to see my breast and waited impatiently as I struggled to undo my gown. I could barely move but pulled clumsily and in pain at the snaps. He looked it over briefly, giving the residents time to stare at a mastectomy with expander placement. He again said it looked great and that I would go home that morning. As he was walking away I called out, "Excuse me, if you could please snap my gown closed!" He fumbled with the task and left as I was there feeling humiliated and dehumanized being put on display like that to those residents. I felt totally discounted by his egotistical manner and assumptions. I was enraged at this level of objective treatment when I was suffering at such a deep physical and emotional level. He could have, at least, asked how I felt rather than just giving me his opinion that I looked good! The next person to arrive was the cancer surgeon. I asked why she was there that morning as I knew she was leaving that day for a conference in Paris. She smiled and said she would be flying out later. In her quiet and steady way, she also expressed again how good I looked and that I would go home that day. She said the surgery went very well. I also told her I had had a bad reaction to medication, but she just shook her head and said "good-by" and that she would see me in two and a half weeks. Ugh! The plastic surgeon was next to arrive, again saying how good I looked! This was really hard to believe after what I had gone through the night before. I had broken blood vessels under my eyes from all the vomiting! But she said, "Oh yes, you have that certain look. You'll be fine." That was comforting but, again, more of an objective observation than any real communication. I asked her if I was, indeed, on morphine the night before referring again to the bad medication reaction. She affirmed it was morphine, but, like the rest of them, my previous rough evening was news to her. Didn't any of these people read the chart before they saw the patient? A while later, I heard a supervising doctor in the hall reviewing my case to a group of residents or students. He mentioned the medication I was on, and it was not morphine. I began wondering if there had been a mix-up in medications or a possible overdose reaction. I knew one of the leading causes of death in our country was from medical interventions. From Wikipedia, I read there were an estimated 44,000 to 98,000 deaths per year from adverse effects of complications caused by or resulting from medical intervention. From other sources, I read that was a very conservative estimate. I was determined to piece together the facts to protect myself from a similar experience the next time I might undergo a surgery. Thank goodness my family was there to observe, question, and advocate for me! Thank goodness they were assertive and that those "Amazon" women got what they needed done!

As the morning progressed, I gingerly took my first walk to the bathroom. I monitored my own medication doses. I expressed fluid from a bulb that was collecting fluid from a tube inserted into my chest wall. I had very little contact with the day nurse even for assistance to wash up. The pain was tremendous… "the pressure of a car sitting on my chest" could describe it. When I asked for help, a male nurse's assistant brought in a package with a disposable washcloth, towel, and packaged soap. I was basically one-handed, and while I stared at the package he had left on the bed, I knew it was time to go home. There was no real care left here. Several visitors arrived, and Gary's presence helped me rise to the effort to converse, but it was hard. I was so weak and out of it. I put on one of the pretty front closing tops my thoughtful sisters had bought me. With Gary's help, I slowly and cautiously made it out to the car and back to our beautiful home. Luckily enough, codeine and muscle relaxants helped me tolerate the activity just long enough to get home and to sleep for a few hours. My two good friends arrived with loving emotional support and flowers. Their presence uplifted me and kept me wrapped in the security of love and care. I am amazed by how the endorphins of love really keep pain and depression at bay. You can really only be in one emotion at a time, and, for me, the consistent outpouring of love and attention was so helpful and appreciated.

It must have hastened my recovery as well because within four days I was backing off the doses of narcotics and using more Tylenol for pain control. The week was kind of blurry with calls, cards, simple meals, and lots of sleep. The most poignant time I remember was sitting on the recliner chair watching the birds come to the bird feeder. Their gentle spirits seemed soothing. The house was quiet that week with my daughter Christy off on a vacation with cousins and grandparents. Gary was there for a couple days, then off to work, and I was alone. The quiet of nature surrounding me was a powerful force in bringing me back to life. We had been in our house only a year, and it was a beautiful setting on a hill a few blocks from Puget Sound. We were surrounded by a variety of trees and flowers all in bloom the first of July. The animals and birds happily humming around me seemed a true blessing and all together created a healing retreat.

Chapter 5

Affirmation of Spirit

Within two weeks of recovery, I began thinking about "affirmation" and what it could mean for me. Could I affirm I would eventually recover vitality, energy, beauty, faith? ... I knew I needed help energetically. From the effects of anesthesia and various medications, I felt disconnected from everything. I felt in the world but not quite all there at the same time. I had met a woman through work who did Reiki for people after surgery, and gave her a call. Reiki is a therapy that involves the practitioner sending healing life force or energy through their hands into the energy field of the subject to facilitate healing. We set up four treatments for that first week, at her recommendation. Each session helped me regain a connection to my physical reality. Each session brought me to a peaceful place where I could begin to breathe gently without pain as it gradually lessened the intense pressure over my chest. With each session, I experienced physical relief from pain and, gradually, gained more vitality. I began to perform my bathing and grooming with more ease and less discomfort as well as showing some interest in communicating. I began to write thank-you cards and e-mails to the beautiful people who had supported me over the past couple months. Words of appreciation for their support brought encouragement to me that my recovery would continue, and I was so appreciative of their presence in my life.

The following Thursday was the day for me to call for the pathology report. I had time to rest, heal, write, and contemplate. I called early that morning to find the results of the pathology on the breast tissue dissected from my chest wall. I was shaking and scared and trying to put away memories of conversations on results that had all been so devastating: the abnormal mammogram and abnormal biopsy. The lumpectomy had also been devastating as they had found abnormal cells within the margins of the dissected tissue and abnormal cells throughout and not just on the suspected calcifications. In the back of my mind, I now worried they might find malignant cells in the tissue from the mastectomy that would warrant chemo and radiation. If that happened, it might even require the removal of the expander placed for the initial phase of reconstruction. On the other hand, somewhere that fear of more cancer was not strong. So, with slightly shaky hands and tremulous voice, I called for the result. I was again alone as Gary and Christy had gone off for the week camping. The nurse took some time to respond but finally came back with the results. The pathology examination of the tissue found no DCIS, no malignant cells, no precancerous cells, no abnormal cells at all!

In that moment, everything came rushing into and back to me as if my life the past two months suddenly had clarity and meaning. In the month of waiting for the mastectomy, my cancer was healed! I was healed and restored. My first reaction was that I had cut my breast off for nothing! If abnormal cells had not been found, that meant my treatments and life style changes the past two months had been enough to reverse whatever was left, or, my immune system had kicked in and resolved the remaining abnormal cells, or both! My next thought was that I would have only seen this demonstration of the power to heal if I had cut out the breast because isolated abnormal cells left were not detectable on a mammogram! It was a perfect outcome for me to see the power of natural medicine, the power of healing touch, the power of love, and, most importantly, the power of God's grace. I had struggled so, especially in the beginning, with the knowledge that I had developed breast cancer. How I could have faith in my medicine when I had used so much of the knowledge, the foods, herbs, and homeopathies that I thought would help me stay healthy? Receiving the diagnosis of breast cancer had made me feel that if my healing approach had let me down like this, then, it did not work. After receiving the proof from the labs that I was cancer free my faith was restored. Everything I had done had helped to realize such a good outcome, and my passion and affirmation for Nature's power to heal were overflowing!

Chapter 6

Humility

My joy, relief, and affirmation of faith continued for several days. I called my family and friends with the good news of the biopsy report that showed absolutely no cancer cells had been detected and that I was cancer free. Again, I expressed my thanks to them for their presence and assistance in my life and this journey.

Gary and Christy went camping that second week of my recovery. I had encouraged them to go as it was an annual trip with other families we looked forward to each year. I knew we all needed a break from the stress we had been going through, but, perhaps in hindsight, I didn't or couldn't ask for what I really needed. I think I took pride in being pretty tough. I had toughed it out when I was sick in the past, did natural child birth and cared for many people who were sick. I felt confident I could handle it. However, I was still pretty shaky from the intensity of pain and still very weak. I hadn't started any walks and wasn't driving yet. I had a recent episode where I had asked Gary to call and check up on me that 4th of July while at a family picnic. I didn't hear from him for seven hours. I tried to call him but he never picked up. Apparently cell coverage was bad, and he hadn't thought about using a land line. It was only a couple days after surgery, and I had a small anxiety attack. I guess it had shaken my confidence. This time, before they left for this camping trip, I tried to emphasize how vulnerable I still felt and needed to be reassured they would be checking in with me fairly often. I was pretty sure I could handle it but was also aware how physically and emotionally traumatized I felt from the whole ordeal. My breast still felt like the weight of a bag of cement was sitting on it. I could hardly move my left arm without aggravating the pain and pressure over my chest, and I was so tired even just after a shower or preparing a meal. I had tried driving but was limited in the use of one arm. Soon after they left, I felt so alone and abandoned. My emotions were still raw, and it didn't take much to bring me to tears. Looking back, I'm sure my shakiness and emotions were also a result of lots of medications still clearing from my system. Nevertheless, I was definitely feeling vulnerable, lost, lonely, and needy.

Several days into their camping trip was when I received the good news my prayers were answered. I was cancer free with absolutely no cancer found in the breast tissue! This also meant no reason for radiation and chemotherapy. I waited all day for them to call. I received no calls in the morning, one missed call in the afternoon and none later in the evening. It was such a disappointment not to be able to share with them the positive result. I grew hurt and angry the more time went by and they hadn't checked up on me. I was gradually becoming possessed by an old childhood wound of abandonment and could feel myself going to the dark side with self-pity and anger. Gary finally reached me a couple days later, and I gave him a good raking over the coals. Eventually, I told him the good news but with little response on his end. Perhaps he was hurt at my criticism or anger expressed about not calling, but the news about the cancer being gone was taken like old news. His reaction to me seemed to be that he had expected this result. He didn't express or share the relief and gladness that I had anticipated and expected. It was, needless to say, anticlimactic and disappointing to feel this lack of connection again at probably the best news of my life, about our life together, and about our future.

When they got home that Sunday night, the pent-up resentment and hurt let loose. I found out Gary hadn't even told Christy, or what he told her didn't mean the same as what I had relayed to him. They told me about their trip and gave me some details but not once did they congratulate me or hug me or even ask how I was doing. That certainly could have been because they could feel the sour mood I was in. Then, something snapped in me. I had it with what I interpreted as their apathy and neglect! I lost my temper and let them have it. I started screaming and ranting about what the positive biopsy result meant to me and how it hurt to have them be so nonchalant or disinterested in my outcome or well-being. I asked Gary if he was going to bail on me emotionally and physically if I had to go through this again. I screamed at my daughter that I couldn't imagine any of her friends not even asking their mom how they were doing after surgery or express any happiness at such good outcomes. That's when I found out Gary hadn't even bothered to tell her, and that only fueled my rage. They put me off with excuses and tried to walk away from me until I started throwing things. A rage of emotion exploded, and I lost control. Neither one of them seemed to be able to offer the care I needed them to express for me! Of course, it would be rather difficult to be caring to someone who was so angry and on the attack!

Later, crying and feeling hurt, abandoned, deflated, and ashamed at my actions, I tried to sort out what had happened to me. In the midst of the most powerful evidence of God's love, I felt totally abandoned. Their actions had triggered an old childhood wound I had suffered with before, and I had gotten sucked into a familiar black hole of sadness and anger. How could I hold such parallel realities at the same time? With such gratitude in my mind for my eventual good outcomes, how could I also feel such loneliness, rage, and anger? Some time and compassion eventually brought me through this inner turmoil of conflicted anger, hurt, and guilt. Insight and compassion for me, for Gary, and for Christy helped me accept the different ways we each dealt with this scary time. Gradually, my emotional reactions quieted. I had been just as mean as I could be to the people I loved most, and yet I knew my physical healing was real, and I was loved deeply to have received it. There was only one explanation for my healing from the surgery and cancer. I recognized it as an expression of God's Grace. A lesson I had to learn earlier in my life was taken in again. In accepting my darker emotions and having compassion for where they came from, somehow through God's unconditional love, I was able to experience such love for all of us.

My life has had repeated opportunities for learning this lesson of God's unconditional love, and the lesson had helped me find some freedom through self-acceptance. I tried to be the perfect good girl when I was young: straight-A student, popular, thin, pretty etc. But trying to keep that up nearly killed me as I developed unhealthy relationships with food and my body in the form of serious eating disorders. I learned that those obsessions were really a coping mechanism to help me escape the feelings that came as a result of conscious and subconscious thoughts. I learned that as I became aware of what my beliefs were that created those emotions, I could practice new beliefs and experience more emotional freedom. Through Grace, I recovered from those eating disorders and found a vitality and passion for life I had never had before. As I grew emotionally and spiritually, recovering from those struggles, it seemed a miracle I was brought into more life-affirming relationships, meaning, joy, and opportunity to serve others. I got my master's degree at Antioch in psychology when in my 20's. I was empowered by achieving that goal. It could only have happened through the support of loved ones. I had one girlfriend in particular who really encouraged me and believed I could do it. It was the first realization of a dream through the power of visualization, prayer, and faith. I had lived my life to that point trying to meet other's expectations. But, I had finally learned to listen to and follow my own heart's desire! Despite my good work ethic and intelligence, I had had very little confidence in myself to perform adequately. My perfectionism and obsessive nature created a perception I was always inadequate and fell short in my achievement. There were some other rough growing experiences along the way that created opportunities for personal growth and self-awareness. I had experienced unsatisfactory relationships, including a physically abusive one; relationship issues with a boss at a job; and my husband's cancer and death. However, each of these eventually offered motivation and information to make changes. I practiced surrendering to the experience as a practice in my faith and a willingness to believe the experience could be a lesson with a positive outcome. I worked diligently with various therapists to uncover the thoughts and feelings, conscious and unconscious, contributing to my problem. I learned that those thoughts and feelings projected to the world around me created familiar responses that reinforced my conscious and subconscious beliefs. Once I became aware of them, compassionately faced and accepted them, then my life began to express what I wanted and, more importantly, I was capable of receiving or taking it in. My wonderful first husband, my beautiful daughter, my experience as a mother, finding another amazing man to share my live with, and my naturopathic degree, were one testament after another that my life was being guided on a path of healing.

The positive growth in my life was also an opportunity to demonstrate and share my faith. My belief that God is Love and that love is letting go of fear, had taken me on a path of self-awareness. When each challenge arose, I asked the question: "What am I afraid of?" A brilliant Jungian therapist led me in the questioning, and it reshaped my belief system about me and my place in the world. Instead of fears, rejection, self-criticism, or not enough love, I started developing a belief that I was already whole and complete. I tried to believe I was a unique expression of God. Each time I had doubt, fear, or anger I would ask and face the subconscious belief that contradicted my conscious intention. My amazingly skilled analyst worked with my dreams to help me hear and feel the awakening parts of my personality as well as the emotions of past traumas and neglect. I tell my patients that we do not really get rid of any part of us but grow into parts that more accurately reflect our wholeness.

When our soul can hold unconditional love and regard for all of us.... including all of our darkest behaviors and feelings, then we have arrived to the individuation of the soul. Jung described individuation as the processes through which differentiated components become integrated into stable wholes.

Finding my cancer gone and totally healed was a gift that immensely strengthened my faith and commitment to live my life even more from my faith and passion. I was being given more time and another chance to live fully. However, even more important and astounding was the ability for Gary, Christy, and I to work through our hurts, fear, and anger and to see the healing power of love bring understanding, care, and connection back to our relationships. It took a while to get back on track. After several talks together, we gained perspective and were able to express and receive the care each of us felt for one another. With my own inner turmoil projecting my need for care but unable to ask or receive it, I was not able to see how they were going through this, too. When Gary pointed this out to me, I started to understand that withdrawing was their attempt to protect themselves from me and their own fears. They started giving to me when I started asking for what I needed. Most importantly, from being able to face those past feelings of neglect, abandonment, and unworthiness, I withdrew the projection that I was being treated that way by the people who loved me. I could now receive their love offered and really take in the love that was always there.

Chapter 7

Recovery

With such a good outcome, it was surprising how difficult the process of recovery still turned out to be. The immediate few weeks of intense pain and weakness gradually improved. Though each day was better than the last, my spirit still struggled. I had ups and downs in my moods. The feeling of being uncared for and alone lingered and repeatedly surfaced when pain returned or intensified. At the same time, I also felt deeply relieved and grateful to know the cancer was gone. It took weeks of working through my disgruntled state to eventually find some acceptance and compassion for all of us, where I started enjoying life as a family including the projects and activities that energized and bonded us. We felt and expressed our love to one another, and it was stronger for what we had gone through together. Our love for one another was really stronger than ever.

A big contribution to the depression during my recovery was the grief in losing my beautiful breast. It probably seemed less significant to Gary, Christy, and others because I was going through "reconstruction." The reconstruction for me, however, only intensified the loss. Each time I looked at this thing, the temporary expander, inside my chest and the ugly scars, I was shocked and even sickened. It took a long time to come to acceptance. As the process seemingly dragged on, I knew intellectually it would probably turn out looking okay, but I could not imagine I would ever really feel whole or normal again. The pain persisted for months, and even though I was functioning, the constant pain was a reminder of what I had gone through. It was so difficult holding the emotions and internal drama as I went through my day-to-day activities.

Visits to the plastic surgeon were disturbing because at first the nurses seemed superficial, too busy, and impersonal. I had doubts that I had picked the right plastic surgeon. She and her staff reassured me I was healing very well, but I was worried about everything. The expander implant felt like it was too big as it extended from the center of my chest to under my armpit. I later learned it had slipped to the side, but that was not significant to them because it would all be corrected in the next surgery... eight months later. The scar from the drain tube, in place for five days, was worse than the mastectomy incision across my breast. I started using an essential oil blend a friend had sent me to soften the skin and heal the scar. I sent my body loving messages as I massaged the oil into the wound hoping that would add another level of healing to my spirit and cells.

Two weeks after the mastectomy and expander placement, I went in to have the stitches removed, and the nurse was ready to begin the expansion. The expansion was a process that involved injecting the implant gradually (over months) with saline. The expansion process facilitated the growth of new tissue to accommodate an implant. Once it got to the right size, it would remain in place for six weeks or so. Next, another surgery would be needed to replace the expander with the permanent prosthesis. Two weeks post mastectomy, I was still in quite a lot of pain and told the nurse I was under the impression we wouldn't begin expansion until the third week. The nurse was happy with how it looked and began to set up the materials. A steady voice inside me came out. Without reservation, I told her that I would prefer to wait a week. She was a little taken aback, but conceded; blowing it off that she did this procedure twenty times a week, and it was just no big deal. Well, for me, still burning and stinging from pain and just barely beginning to use my arm with some strength and breathing without a stabbing pain over my heart... it was a big deal! I needed to speak up for myself and not step backwards in my recovery. When the doctor came in, I told her I had decided to wait a week, and she quickly agreed another week was more appropriate. Her response validated my intuition, and I was proud of myself for taking care of myself in that instance!

My surgeon was undergoing breast reconstruction herself. She had found cancer in both breasts. She would also be required to undergo chemotherapy. Her experience with breast cancer gave her much more compassion and insight, and that was one of the reasons I had chosen her as my surgeon. She not only had years of experience as a reconstructive surgeon, she also knew and communicated first-hand understanding of the process we were both going through. It really helped me to feel understood. I had a lot of anger and often projected this onto the doctor and her staff. I realized I had better work on my critical attitude toward them because I would be seeing them each week for months during the reconstructive process. As the pain subsided, so did my anger and critical attitude. When my attitude changed a funny thing happened: the nurses turned out to be not so bad after all! We started communicating better, and I even began to appreciate the primary nurse as the one person in the office interested in my naturopathic approaches. She encouraged my natural supports and acknowledged their benefit in my recovery. Besides being cancer-free, I had no infections, had healthy skin that was growing, my energy and immune system were good, and scar-healing was progressing with optimal outcome.

On a practical basis, however, I had to find something to cover this "thing", the temporary prosthesis, so I could wear my clothes. It became a challenge to find baggy tops that hid my lumpy and lopsided chest. My usual lightly structured underwire bra dug right into the implant. I was numb over the area so I couldn't tell if it was cutting into the skin or applying too much pressure. My old bra just was not a good fit. I tried various bras looking for something without the underwire and large enough to hold the breast that was drifting laterally under my armpit. It was amazing to me that neither surgeon had given me much help on what to do about this. It was so typical of medical doctors to discuss only the pertinent information related to their intervention. I eventually found a couple padded bras that would cover the implant and its weird shape. I also added pads of different sizes to the other side to even out the discrepancy in size. Needless to say, it probably appeared to some people that I was already looking pretty good! The thing was, I had been small my whole life, nearly a B with light padding, so a 36B to a 34C felt rather awkward and bulky. It also felt phony, and somehow minimized the wound that was so present to me.

I came to realize that women have different attitudes about their breasts. I guess I had never really thought about it before. My sister-in-law had wanted hers enhanced, and I had thought that was probably to help her self-esteem and to feel attractive, having lost her shape after nursing a couple babies. My sister told me she didn't really think it would matter to her to lose a breast until I lost mine, and then she realized maybe she did feel they were a part of her self-image. A friend with large breasts definitely communicated they were a part of her identity as a woman and an aspect of her beauty. An Asian woman, who was smaller than me, said she would not miss hers at all as you probably wouldn't even be able to tell. I became aware my relationship to my breast was a unique, personal journey. My women friends could listen and have empathy, but each woman had a different attitude. Of course, I tried to remind myself that my attitude may have changed having lost a breast, so I tried to remember what it had been before.

I was always a very feminine woman. I was voted "most feminine" senior year of high school. I had always been slender, except for maybe junior high, and pretty happy with my breasts. They were small but perky, and with a little light padding, support, or underwire, seemed proportionate to my body. I was slender on top through the neck, arms, and chest and a little fuller in the hips and thighs. I had gone through an anorexic stage in my late teens and had recovered much more balance with body image, but I still liked being slender. I am sure the desire to be slender motivated my healthy diet and good nutrition. My Chinese doctor discussed a theory that anorexics don't want to menstruate or come fully into womanhood. At first, I thought that theory did not seem true for me. I thought just the opposite. I feel I was lured into anorexia by the desire to fit the image of female beauty projected by corporate media. Stick thin models and actresses were what I saw as beautiful women. I remember in junior high school looking at models in magazines and comparing my body to theirs. I always felt overweight and inadequate in comparison. It dawned on me that the parts I noticed and compared were weight, thighs, hair, and skin. Breasts were not on my list of things I wished to change or improve.

I wondered where I may have gotten other negative and positive messages or attitudes about my body.   My mom had frequently dieted, and my dad worked out regularly to keep trim.   There were definitely messages there about maintaining a healthy weight.   I had acne and had been very self-conscious about my skin.   My mom had psoriasis so definitely there was negative attention to skin problems in the family.   Mom didn't like her thin hair and complained about it.   She complimented my thick long hair so I had positive attention for that.   My mother had smaller breasts, but she was always positive about that. My best friend in high school had very large breasts, and she definitely got attention for that, but never once did I envy or wish they were mine.   I did not fill out a bathing suit very well so had to look for certain styles.   Anything braless looked bad as I needed some help to have a shape! On the other hand, braless around the house was easy and comfortable. I learned how to make the most of what I had and appreciated my breasts.

My grief over losing my breast became another window of opportunity to self-discovery. The classic image of Venus coming out of the water touching a breast kept coming to me. It was an image I had painted some years before. It felt very much like a self-portrait at the time and now had more meaning about my self-image regarding my breast. She was built much like me with soft round hips and more slender upper body. Her breasts were small but round and supple with a beautiful erect nipple. In the picture, she is touching her nipple, and it looked to me erotic and powerful. I identified with those two adjectives. I loved the sensuality of this feminine image of Aphrodite, and the power it contained. She had been a strong archetype for me and was present in my home, art, clothing, and dreams.

In relationships, my breasts were a strong erogenous zone. Despite their smaller size, I enjoyed the sensation and pleasure they gave me. I also enjoyed how they pleased my partner and provided for his pleasure as much as my own. Though I was nearly fifty years old just before my breast surgery, I was learning to appreciate and enjoy them sexually more than ever before. My partner Gary brought out sensuality in me that was fun and satisfying. The relationship offered me more self-acceptance and pleasure than I had ever had before. This new "tragedy", in the beginning, seemed to hit hard in this area of body image and self-acceptance. I remember the night before my mastectomy hoping we would make love, anticipating it would be my last time feeling whole and complete in my body. Gary was not interested. I think he was more concerned about what the next morning would bring. A couple weeks after the mastectomy, we made love for the first time without my breast, and I cried the whole time. The tears came from the acute awareness of having lost the body I had so thoroughly learned to enjoy with him. My sense of beauty, femininity, and childlike playfulness were lost with my tears from the removal of that breast. John Grey, the author of __Women Are from Venus, Men Are from Mars,__ said that if you are the only naked woman in the room, to the man, you are the Goddess! That was exactly how I had felt with Gary, and I wondered if that would ever come back.

Reconstruction eventually helped but not in the beginning. I remember when I was told I needed the mastectomy that the surgeon threw out the "reconstruction" word. It sounded hopeful and even nice to think I could end up looking normal, maybe even better than before. I never thought I would choose to have implants, but since it was the only reconstruction option for me, it seemed like something good could come out of this. The plastic surgeon said reconstruction would be painful, and I could imagine from the look of the expander it would be awkward during the expansion stage. Another reason I had chosen this plastic surgeon was that the expander she used was about half the size of the other doctor's. However, it was the expander placement that caused most of the excruciating pain immediately after the mastectomy because it was placed in newly traumatized tissue. Each week following the surgery, I had to go back to have it injected with more saline. Although the pain gradually subsided, each weekly visit to fill it with saline caused a relapse of pain. It usually lasted about 48 hours but was so similar to the initial trauma that despite my attempts to have a good attitude, my mood would plummet. The pain and also the placement of the implant was a constant source of irritation and discomfort. They finally conceded that the implant had shifted off to the side and that had caused added stress to the muscles as well as the difficulty to find any kind of bra to fit. I knew this was temporary, but my day-to-day struggle to accept this was so difficult.

I hit a low point about week four into the expansion feeling depression, anger, pain and fear. Gary could not relate or understand my problem, and his attempts to tell me I looked good to him or that others could not notice, did not help. I called my sister Sue one day and asked her to join me for coffee. I wanted to plan a women's gathering to thank the women who had supported my healing over the previous months. When she asked how I was doing, I expressed my feelings of struggling with my shape and with the limitation in what I could wear. She suggested we go to Nordstrom's and look for a bra. I had heard they help with prosthesis for mastectomies but wondered what they could have for lopsidedness during this expansion phase. Sue suggested we go into the dressing room and look at what we had to work with. When I revealed my breasts, her expression took on a look of surprise, concern, horror, grief, and then tears. Gentle tears rolled down her cheeks, and, in that moment, she expressed the compassion I needed most. It seems I needed her to express those feelings so I could accept them myself. Instead of being brave and strong, I had to accept the horror of all the cutting up and deformity. Her honesty helped me find that compassion I needed to find in myself. Sue told me I was perfectly normal to feel sad, angry, hurt, and afraid! Even though I tried to tell myself how much worse it could be, she reassured me this was bad enough! She had a way of being with me in one of my darkest places, and it was like a door opened to the light. We got ourselves together and went out of the dressing room to look for a bra. I asked a young salesgirl if she could help fit me having had a mastectomy. She looked a little flustered and ran off to get the one woman who was trained to help women needing prosthesis. In the meantime, Sue found a bra that looked like a possibility. It was lightly structured, had no under wire and was wide on the sides. The salesperson trained as a fitter joined us, and she, too, looked at what we were dealing with. It seemed she had seen mastectomies but not many expanders, and she soon realized the challenge. The bra Sue found fit really well! We padded the other side, and I looked almost even. The bra was beige, not white, which also visually helped even out the picture. I started breathing and realized for the first time that I felt like a woman again. It was an amazing emotional and physical shift of acceptance.

I began some body work about this time with a therapist that combined massage and Tai Wan Do acupressure. This body work continued to help me with the integration.

She gave me tools to use. She recommended I talk to my tissue about this reconstruction process. She suggested I thank my breast for going through this with me and for the ability to make this transformation. She used her intention and touch skills to work with the implant and around the traumatized tissue to bring relaxation and integration of this foreign object into my energetic and physical body. She also helped move out toxicity, and, surprisingly, I was often a little sick after the treatments. The detoxification treatment was definitely a great benefit for clearing the drugs used before and after surgery. At some point about five weeks after the mastectomy, I began to have periods during the day when I felt whole and not even aware of the "brick" sitting on my chest.

Christy's younger cousin Shelby came to spend an overnight, and I wanted to show her my implant. My philosophy with Christy had been to be as open as was useful and try not to hide or cover up what was really going on. This was definitely still going on, at least for me! I talked about it a little with Shelby and told her about the reconstruction. I asked her if she wanted to see it, and she did. I showed her the breast and had her feel its hardness. She seemed a little dismayed and said "That's too bad for people who hug you." I laughed and realized it was a little scary for her, but, in her quick wit, she had summed it up nicely! I started to lighten up more often and began allowing some of the acceptance stage of grief to penetrate my perspective.

Chapter 8

Birth of the Black Baby

Nearly three months after my mastectomy, I had a dream that I was riding a bike lost in a city and that I rode passed a black man holding a black baby. He was saying to a young black woman something about getting fresh water.

About two months after surgery, I became aware of how angry I was. I was angry to be going through a cancer experience again! I was also angry at having to deal with a medical system that was so cut off emotionally. My cancer surgeon was the best at her skill in surgery but rarely, with me, able to communicate anything personally related to my emotional experience. I had volunteered some history to her on my first office visit, but it felt like that created even more of a barrier to connect emotionally.

The nurses were generally efficient yet there seemed to be a rule not to talk to the patient like a "normal person" as a way to maintain a professional emotional boundary. Surgery was similar. I remember sitting in the pre-surgery room for three hours until the IV nurse finally came around to insert a needle that would be used for the anesthetic. As she worked, she said that this would probably be the thing I would remember hurting the most and then proceeded to jab the needle into my arm, twisting it in place until tears welled up in my eyes. I asked her to pull it out a little, but she had already taped it up efficiently and expressed pleasure at how it looked. How it felt to me was not given any significance. Over and over again the "care" provided was based on how it looked or how well it followed procedure and had almost nothing to do with how I felt or experienced the procedure. From my traumatic drug reaction after the mastectomy surgery to the pain with reconstruction, "my feeling experience" of the interventions was considered subjective, according to the medical model that valued only objective outcomes. Each episode brought up feelings of being discounted and unheard and, perhaps, even emotionally abandoned. It also brought up anger from what my first husband had gone through with his cancer experience in the medical system from multiple blunders regarding his care to the lack of sensitivity by the medical system. The dark anger that kept erupting felt like it was the cause of my fatigue, low mood, and lack of motivation for daily activities. I would go to the weekly expansion visits angry about being in constant pain and not being able to sleep, but I also became aware that there was much more underneath. It wasn't until the pain started lifting that I was more in touch with what had consumed me.

Hurricane Katrina hit in the midst of my reconstruction. Many people in our country were forced into grappling with this devastating crush to humanity even as I was still suffering through my own personal trials. There seemed to be an increased awareness of suffering and neglect that permeated our country. "Suffering" and "neglect" were words that seemed to fit what I was going through. I was having my personal experience of both so was able to feel compassion and understanding. I could identify with survivor rage, even condone in some way the anger that was projected by the people looting and shooting at the government helicopters that were trying to rescue people. The rage at neglect and at denial of their physical and emotional needs was so poignant in those images. My strong emotional response to the suffering and anger of these people stirred in me memories of my dream of the black baby. I could see that the dream image of the "black baby" represented the emergence to consciousness of my rage and anger from childhood, of my perception of events with my first husband's medical treatment and death, as well as my current experience. The depth and origin of these feelings had been kept unconscious but were now very raw and real. This dark baby was a shadow image of some aspect of me suppressed or hidden in the unconscious. The image available in a dream and its associations were now revealing those feelings so it was time to face and deal with them. I couldn't keep them repressed, any longer...

My anger kept resurfacing, and I was really drawn to watch on television the violence and brutality after Hurricane Katrina. The expression of hurt and injustice of the people of New Orleans fit my projection of anger toward the medical system's impersonal, objectified and sometimes barbaric interventions. As I wrote this, there was trepidation going into it because of the intensity of anger and pain I felt. Why was my reaction to neglect so huge? Certainly it tapped into my personal wound from childhood. Physical and emotional neglect seemed to have impacted me significantly. The experience I was in currently was reactivating childhood pent-up feelings of anger, grief, low self-esteem, and disempowerment I had never actualized at the time. It had gotten trapped! My experience now was triggering the past that caused my reaction to lash out, become depressed, and lose hope. Healing from this would be a journey of transformation... However, facing those feelings and withdrawing the projection would take time and assistance. I had learned over the years that thinking "when am I going to be passed this?" is a waste of time. I had learned that once the unconscious source of the feelings was identified, time was needed for me to come to a place of understanding, compassion, and acceptance of my feelings. I needed support and guidance to get to there but was motivated out of a knowing that emotional freedom from my anger and sadness were around the corner if I surrendered and truly faced those very feelings.

The black baby of my dream represented to me my shadow. In Jungian terms, the shadow is any aspect of your psyche that is suppressed or undeveloped. Anger and pain too difficult to face until now were surfacing. There was also a positive male and female figure emerging within that could hold me in this process of waking up or becoming conscious in regards to this anger and pain. These figures were also shadow images. My internal Mother and Father were evolving from this experience so that my conscious self had more of a capacity to love myself and accept the depth of my emotions, even those of rage and anger. Fresh water represented the new emotional capacity to hold the darker emotions. Jung termed the process of individuation as bringing parts of the immature psyche into an integrated whole to form a stable personality. Besides awakening these difficult feelings, I wondered if this would lead to more stability.

My anger would surface most easily with my thirteen year old daughter. I certainly needed more of that stability dealing with her! She definitely was asserting herself more readily, and her feedback to me was often in a condescending tone of voice. I could usually get passed that, but something else about her seemed to trigger some deeper anger. I could hear it in my tone of voice and in my attempt to control and criticize her. Of course, intellectually, I knew this was not helping, and the last thing I wanted was to push her away. Still, I seemed unable to change my reactions. Something like possession would take over, and my "witch" would surface again with her. I was beginning to feel desperate, as I knew that love can be damaged and also how vulnerable we can be to significant events in our life. I feared Christy would grow to hate me, and our relationship would be negatively impacted forever.

One day, I brought the writing to my mentor with some effort, because I was not feeling very productive. What was most on my mind was this anger that I kept projecting on to Christy. My mentor asked me a pivotal question: "What happened to you at thirteen years old?" "That was the year my struggle with depression began," I replied. We had moved that year. I was starting junior high school. My mom and dad, parents of five kids, were both starting new jobs. This all seemed partially to contribute, but really didn't explain the dark place I had gone to at that time. My mentor then led me through a guided imagery where I met myself at thirteen. She came to me easily, and the reunion was comforting. However, what she did next was the surprise. She told me that I had cut myself off from the zest of life and enthusiasm that Christy possessed. I had left behind, at thirteen years old, those qualities that Christy possessed and expressed so easily. I had this realization that what I reacted to in Christy was what was missing for me, and it was something I dearly grieved. Feeling too much responsibility had cut me off from the sweetness and wonder of life. It came with such clarity that at that age, for various reasons, I had fallen from innocence and taken on adult responsibilities. I had assumed it meant doing it by myself and that it all depended on me....that I was unsupported. That equated to a huge burden and fear I associated with responsibility. Being fairly capable and smart, I could and did succeed in taking on responsibility, but in many ways I had suffered. It happened especially at times of crisis such as the diagnosis of my husband's terminal cancer and again with the diagnosis of my own cancer. I realized the suffering was mostly from a disconnect from Spirit and from the innocence of living life with a sense of support, protection, purpose, and destiny. I then began to see through my little agnostic thirteen year old that in observing and reacting to her, I was witnessing connection to Spirit in action! The pain of being separate from my bliss began to lift.

I can't quite express what this meant, only that an old heaviness of mood began to unravel. I quit waking up each morning with a dark cloud to work through. Usually the day would bring my mood up, and I certainly had joy at times, but for so long there was still a heaviness and feeling of depression waiting to fall back. Now, it was like the clearing of a dense fog. There were more episodes of lightness and more trust that life's continuous stream of "miracles" was really the nature of my life, and I could start believing I truly was supported. I felt more open to receive from others, and, most importantly, I could celebrate my Christy's spirit instead of putting her down for it! The communication lightened up for both of us. I knew it was happening when, after several nights, she came to me with homework and then started coming to me with a kiss goodnight. My heart melted. As I was reconnecting with the part of me I had cut off, my daughter was regaining the love she needed most from her mom. This was my resurrection! The black baby in the dream represented both the wound and what was missing. Because it was now "born" or brought to my conscious awareness... I could live and love more wholly than ever!

Chapter 9

The Wedding

In the midst of my surgeries, Gary said several times, "We should be married." We had been together five years, had been living together four years, and after buying our house together the year before, it certainly felt like we were married. We had imagined marrying in September as that was the month we met. I had also imagined marrying in our new house, together with our family and friends and with my daughter Christy standing up for me. For several years, Christy had imagined being my maid of honor with her cousin Shelby as the bride's maid. Christy was really into weddings, and even at 12 years of age, she had her wedding dress design, ring, and flowers already picked out! For her, a wedding was a great event, and even if it was mine, she was all over it!

Well, the first of August we decided to go for it. I was still in the middle of expanding my breast and a little on the fence about going ahead. I decided that if I could find a dress that would accommodate my lopsided breast, it would be a sign. Christy found her dress the first time we went shopping, so that decided it. After buying her dress, we had to go through with it! She looked beautiful and picked out something so classic and feminine. I intuitively knew I would find my dress and even knew the week I would find it. With the decision to go forward with the wedding, something came over me that had never happened to this degree before. It was a deep peace and knowing that all was well, really would be well, and was as it should be. There were many details to work out for the wedding but somehow I knew it would all unfold one step at a time. We set a date, I found a dress, we found a convenient rental company for chairs, my mother and sisters offered the catering as a wedding gift, my sister's store did the flowers, I asked my brother-in-law to do pictures, and we pretty much had the wedding in order.

Preparing for the wedding also included finishing up multiple projects on the house. This also seemed a metaphor. Reconstruction, rejuvenation, identity, retreat, and persona were the words that seemed to describe associations with the physical "house" as well as with my body, psyche, and soul. I created a "meditation/massage" room that was finally a space I could dedicate to the Holy Spirit! The creation of the room felt like the Native American ritual of leaving an offering in thanks for prayers answered as a visible symbol of thanksgiving. I could feel myself more and more being carried by Spirit as to where I put my energy and attention. The heart of the home was becoming visible, and this added to my healing and uplift.. Gary finished a storage shed adjacent to the house. We embellished our yard with flowers and more flowers. The five weekends we had before the wedding were spent mostly on the house, and we had so much fun and satisfactions seeing our house continue to transform into a beautiful living space, into our sanctuary and home.

In the middle of expanding my breast and being so tired, still angry and distraught about how it looked and how painful each procedure was becoming, I decided to slow down the process and wait to finish it until after the ceremony. The last two expansions had been the most painful, and I was afraid that if I kept going, my dress wouldn't fit. My doctor agreed to hold off the expansions for a couple months, and I think she and her nurse were glad to get a break from my complaining and whining at each visit. It was just so scary to go in for those injections and come out with this physical pain that was so reminiscent of the surgery. Sometimes the pain took 48 hours or so to settle down, but the last expansions before the wedding had taken a week to recover. It took a week of vicodin and muscle relaxants, which didn't really seem to touch the pain, but, at least, made the pain tolerable. I also didn't like the constipation and depression caused by the vicodin. It would take days to feel myself, and after each round, I was a little more exhausted. It felt like starting a mountain climb all over again. I read an article about a woman who took care of her husband after a knee surgery. It described her experience from the standpoint of the caregiver. She not only had to take on extra work, she also had to put up with her husband who was so different in pain than the man he was before pain. The companion she could talk over the news with, share stories about the kids with, take walks with, and cuddle with at night was not there anymore, and she really missed him. My heart went out to Gary as I read this, knowing he was in much the same position dealing with me when I was in pain. I was a different person. I, too, missed my old self.

Taking this break was the best thing I could have ever done. I came back to feeling like my old self, definitely more able to find energy, satisfaction, joy, and peace with this process we were into! The wedding was planned outdoors in our yard, and we prayed for good weather. However, I was even able to let go of worry about the weather and trusted it would unfold in a divine plan. The day of the wedding was "picture perfect", and a friend described it as "filled with the song of angels." The ceremony turned out to be an hour late because as my dad was dressing, he came out of the walk- in closet in a dress shirt and shorts saying he couldn't find his pants! We searched high and low, but he realized he'd left them at home and had to drive 30 minutes each way to find the new suit pants. In the meantime, the guests were enjoying visiting and drinks, few even realizing there was a delay. We changed ministers a few days prior to the wedding because my friend, Sister Paulita, became ill. I asked another friend Patrice to officiate, and her presence and power filled the ceremony with the Presence of God. In fact, the angels were present because of the beauty of each and every person that participated. "When two or more are gathered in my presence, there I Am" was a powerful reality on our special day!

Chapter 10

The Other Side of Anger

About six weeks after the mastectomy, I held a women's gathering to honor and connect with those women who had helped me through the journey and my miraculous healing. I felt they were all connected by a web of golden light, and I wanted to give back to them as they had each touched me so deeply. The invitation was to attend "A group of powerful women." My mother, sisters, colleagues, good friends, and even some patients were invited. It was a group of about 15 women, and I was so pleased that nearly everyone invited was able to attend. We shared in a potluck meal which seems such an organic and feminine way to nurture one another. I then gathered the women in my living room and began a ceremony. I use that word because in my preparation there was an intention that the

Holy Spirit would touch each person individually as a way of giving back to them some of the gifts I had received. I also wanted to have some way of offering my testimony to God's power and grace. I began with having each person introduce themselves and talk a little about how we were connected through my experience with cancer. It was also an opportunity for me to acknowledge some of their gifts to the group. It was a group of women with varied interests, backgrounds, and religious beliefs, but I intuitively felt these contacts and connections could be useful to all.

The ceremony proceeded with a symbolic process of each woman choosing a batch of fifteen pieces of various golden ribbons. There were a variety of ribbons to express the individuality of the person choosing, but the consistency of a golden thread ran through each one. We then began tying them together so that in the end each woman had a string of different individual threads representing each woman in the group. While we were doing this, I read excerpts from my book that highlighted some of the lows and highs of my experience. Mostly, I wanted to share what for me was a "miraculous event" even in the midst of my human experience. I knew each of these women individually had at least one personal challenge facing them at the time. Several were financial problems. One woman was struggling in her marriage, another with a loss of self-identity, several with major health worries, and several with recent deaths of close loved ones. Each woman, in her own human experience, was grappling with her own edge of fear or grief or abandonment or ... is it that "edge" where in the midst of the human drama, grace and transformation are possible? What tools could I offer these women other than my experience and faith? I asked each woman to offer to the group her request for assistance and prayers. Asking for one's self was not that easy for most. I shared with the group that during my cancer scare, a good friend told me to ask Jesus for healing. It was a turning point in my recovery as I discovered I had never prayed directly for myself. I was honored and thankful for other's prayers but had never really asked for myself. I learned this was not uncommon for these women either. One woman broke through and asked for what she needed. Others needed help to form the words and open up their hearts to the group. Others wanted to pray for someone else, but I tried to direct the prayer back to them. I became aware later how powerful this was for everyone. An important lesson I learned is that it is only in asking that we can really receive. Our soul and intuitions are given desires and dreams that bring us into our path and to reflect the glory and bounty of God. I learned that other women, like me, often know this for others but find it hard to see it for themselves. What is it about our own growth that holds us

117

back from "shining?" One of my favorite quotes by Marianne Williamson is: "As we let our light shine, we unconsciously give other people permission to do the same. As we are liberated from our own fear, our presence actually liberates others."

It was a glorious day and celebration. Each woman was empowered and connected physically and symbolically to something greater than them. I was amazed at my ability to share my writing without nervousness or being self-consciousness. Moving from that inner place of Spirit seemed easier and more right than ever before. There was no room for the ego, as what was most important and needed was available and present in and through me. This in itself was for me another "miraculous event!" Here I was 48 years old, and Spirit was finally available consistently for several hours to direct my thoughts and words! Amen and thank you God!

Chapter 11

Peace

Finally, my day of surgery to replace the expander with the softer, more natural implant arrived. This was the day I had my breasts augmented, or as Christy would say, "When you got your boob job." I cringed when I heard her say that and would tell her, "It's disrespecting herself to call her breasts boobs." To me, breasts represented an aspect of the Aphrodite archetype, the goddess of beauty and love. I had a friend, who also had a mastectomy but no reconstruction, ask me if I would do it again knowing how much pain I would go through? I said I would but couldn't articulate the reason. This experience and that question prompted me to start to thinking about why I had done it and about the emotions and meaning I associated with my breasts.

For the final surgery, I needed little preparation and felt like I really knew the ropes. This was good and bad. Despite feeling prepared and ready in knowing technically what to expect, the week before surgery, I could feel the anxiety and fear. Knowing what I was going to go through again was much scarier in some ways than not knowing. The sterile environment, the anesthesia risks, the recovery risks from infection, and generally being out of control! However, my good outcomes from the other surgeries were strong assurances, that even with the fear, I would weather this well. My husband, Gary, was a trooper, but even he did not sleep well the night prior to surgery, and I could tell it was hard on him, too. He was a little less humorous and seemed to take the process with humility and seriousness. We really were at the mercy of their "care." (That word again.) My reconstructive surgeon seemed the only medical staff who really met me as a person. Her connection uplifted me and kept me with her. She had pictures I had given her of breasts I liked that morning of surgery, and she seemed genuine in her intentions to use them. What I sensed about her was that in connecting with me, she was connected with herself. I wondered if through her own cancer experience, she would also find that inner queen and begin to honor her life apart from her work and her patients. She gave so much and had taken very little time off during her own cancer treatment. I felt a little guilty for the time and attention I was giving to my cancer recovery process, and DCIS was considered so much less serious or progressed then hers and others. On the other hand, I listened to those internal black parents from my dream that were supporting and lifting me up. I felt assured my choices had been right for me.

As I was rolled onto the surgery table, the anesthesiologist started talking about a Christmas when he was in medical school where he was shopping the night before Christmas for his son. He stopped at a bar with a friend and got loaded. Staggering out of the bar at 6:00 p.m. Christmas Eve, he tried at the last minute to buy a cute puppy in the first store he saw. The shop owner refused to sell it to him. My doctor laughed at the story and asked if he went back and thanked that shop owner, and, of course, he laughed and said no. I said to her that was the difference between women and men. Then I passed out. What an odd thing to hear before you go unconscious! Seemed to be an odd attempt to connect, but the story led me to question who had my life in their hands. The two-hour surgery turned into nearly four, but, of course, I wasn't aware of that. When I awoke, it was again to intense, excruciating pain. The pressure on my chest was like the previous surgery, something like a car sitting on my chest with each piercing breath. The nurse was impatient. I asked when I could see Gary, and she said when I was more awake. He and my mom finally arrived. It was hard to talk and my speech was still slurred from the drugs, but it was the first time I didn't cry waking up from surgery. My emotions had been so intense the previous surgeries; this somehow felt like an extension of the first ones but with hope the outcome less devastating, more redemptive. The others signified such great loss for me, and this one was in some ways my reclaiming my wholeness. Shortly after they got me up in a chair, I started vomiting. The nurse was again impatient. As soon as my pain was under a two out of ten, they wanted me discharged. I was at an eight and vomiting. She wanted to give me another injection of pain medication, and I asked for the pain pill that I would go home with as I knew it didn't make me nauseous. She argued that the shot worked faster and gave me another. I proceeded to vomit for another half hour.

My sister Sue arrived about the time I sat up and my parents had left. She was so tender in bathing my neck with a cool cloth and stroking my back. It gave me the strength to tell the nurse I was ready to go home. Gary went to get the car, and Sue helped me to the wheelchair and started wheeling me down the hall. The nurse was irritated we had taken the lead and grabbed the chair from Sue. Out the door we went, vomit bag in hand, and using it. Sue helped pour me into the car, and we headed for our home. I was so glad to get out of there. I appreciated the work they did but was scared for my life and health when at their mercy!

The first two days were very hard. The pain was intense with every movement, and I could only sleep propped up with pillows. That very first night home there was planned a women's group at my house. The "group of powerful women" had turned into a support group. It was called the

"Women's Network of Light", and we met once a month at my home. I did not want to stop the flow of the group as my surgery date landed on the monthly day we met, so I encouraged the group to still gather. I was upstairs recuperating. My healing that first night was in every way enhanced by that group's love and prayers that came wafting up the stairs into my bed and into my body with the new breast and into my soul.

On the third day, I tried to look under my bandages and onto the top of my breasts. They looked really little. I was immediately depressed. How could I go through all this and come out looking the same! I tried to tell myself to not obsess or fret, but I was so sad and angry. I also realized I was detoxifying from all the drugs and anesthesia. I tried to remind myself about the last two surgeries and that I had hit some low days following them for the same reason. I knew it was true because physically

I was trembling and weak. The same physical trembling and weakness that occurred after my mastectomy and following acupressure massage seemed related to the release of toxins. Despite my mental knowing, the irrational emotional took me over for that day. I was ashamed of myself for being so negative and knew it wasn't helping but also realized in retrospect this was another aspect of grief about the whole experience and post traumatic reaction to another assault on my body.

The fourth morning I decided to unwrap the bandage that was covering my whole upper body. It was a couple days early to be removing the bandage, but it was starting to fall apart anyway and needed to be redone. Like a mummy, I loosened the wrap and let it fall away. I was fitted into an elastic bra similar to a sports bra, and I unlatched the Velcro closures with some difficulty as it still hurt to move both arms in many positions. As it opened to reveal my breasts, I was amazed. I stared at myself with utter astonishment to see real breasts standing up. The left breast had a long lateral incision across the middle, and the right breast a modest incision underneath. But, both those beautiful breasts were smiling at me! Even despite bruising and sores developing from a reaction to the bra material, I looked whole and beautiful! My fears were so relieved, and hope that I would be over this whole thing soon was restored. Gary and I met with the surgeon the next day, and she was very pleased as well. I asked about the large incision on the left. The expander had slid further to the left, nearly under my armpit, so in positioning the soft implant she had to sew down that skin to form a capsule to keep it in place. Apparently, that had turned out to be much more complicated than she anticipated, and she had to open up a much larger incision. I was disappointed by this because my mastectomy scar had healed so remarkably well, but I knew I could use all the oils and supplements at my disposal to get just as good or better result this time. I was finally learning this time that positive attention really helped with good outcomes. My healing journey would continue. At this first follow-up visit, I was told to keep the chest ace wrapped, keep padding to that left side, and to wear a sports bra for at least a month. I still had to practice patience to bring this to completion.

Gary was amazed how real and beautiful my breast looked. I laughed as he was looking at them with me before the doctor arrived on that first follow-up visit... He had that look of desire and interest. I asked later how he would ever be able to enjoy these breasts after all we had been through together. He smiled and said he was enjoying them already. Christy was pleased as well and when I showed them to her she said "they're perfect, Mom." Then she immediately had to show me hers and how pretty they were. I told her we needed to take good care of hers because they were so nice.

Gary and Christy were both very different this time during my recovery, but I was probably different, too. They were very kind and attentive. Christy made some of my meals, would kiss me good-night, and was patient with me when I was preoccupied with attending to my dressings and obsessing about each phase of healing. One day I became worried the left one was too low, another day I began obsessing the tissue was adhering to the implant. My neurotic tendencies never seem to change, but I tried to just do what I could and give myself some time to get through it. I took a week off of work, returning nine days after surgery, which felt like a luxury! On the other hand, the time went so quickly, and I knew that if I could pace myself before getting back to the daily work schedule, it would help me heal, strengthen, and detoxify.

Would I do this again? Yes, it seems this was what I needed to feel free from the cancer. Somehow, this is what I needed to go forward with less fear of a return and less anger for going through it. I knew that it was the right choice for me from the beginning, and it seemed to be true to the end.

My knowledge of what promotes cancer had grown immensely in the past seven months. I had researched and consolidated research on supportive nutrients and herbs and was on an extensive supplement regime. My diet and supplement regime was more finely tuned, and I had become a believer in food based/non synthetic supplements as the most potent and effective way to support and nourish. They seemed to make improvements in how I felt immediately. I had no infections with the multiple surgeries. I stopped having the hot flashes I had for the past two years. My energy, concentration, mood, and sleep were better than ever, and, a week after surgery, the extensive bruises were fading to a pale yellow. On Day Five of recovery from the placement of the implants, I was cleaning house, and on Day Six, I was at church and out to breakfast.

Probably more importantly for long term health, I had started working with my thyroid and liver. I was learning about how estrogen, out of balance with progesterone, can promote cancer and can interfere with thyroid function. As I learned more, it began to make sense as to why my body had become susceptible to cancer and how all the supports I had used were needed. The more I learned and tried to put the puzzle of my own body and health together, the more excited I felt about being capable of treating others.

The approach I took was a Holistic experience, and my healing was encompassing that. I continued work with a therapist, individually and with Gary. Both were invaluable in helping us weather the emotional ups and downs of this rollercoaster cancer experience. Fortunately, it resulted in reassurance of our love and faith in one another. It also gave each of us room for our own experience and some insight and appreciation by each other for the other. The bodywork I received was another strong healing force. It seemed to help the body, on an energetic level, integrate and evolve with the changes I was making.

The week I was home healing, I wrote a friend a condensed version on the impact of the experience. I told her the story of meeting my thirteen year old self and realizing I had lost her and her exuberance for life. I told her that with that realization and intention to reconnect with her in myself and also to celebrate it in Christy, I had amazingly changed my behavior with her. I was no longer unconsciously venting in criticism or anger but much more gentle and honestly more supportive. It was undoubtedly the greatest miracle in this whole thing. What I lost at thirteen years old was lost again when Chuck died and again amplified with this breast diagnosis. I was at a point of having to wake up or see this diagnosis take hold of me and cause me to become more fearful, more compulsive, and more rigid. Instead, the process helped me realize I can be awake and trust even more in the challenges. I learned that the challenges can truly hold a blessing if I look for the meaning and pay attention to my story along the way. My guiding light seems to be to find, and even fight for, the connection with the ones I love and even more so with the ones I don't love very easily. I found a peace with the medical establishment, as barbaric as it can be, because their skills helped me find recovery and even physical wholeness. There were limitations in care and connection; especially, with the structure and mechanics of hospital medicine Many individuals, however, brought attention, patience, kindness, and generosity into their work with patients.

Finding some healing in that anger I had carried so long about my husband's experience in allopathic medicine during his lung cancer was really another miracle. I did not expect to find it, but it was really the first thing that came up for me when I was diagnosed. I remember thinking that my experience might be different than his. In some ways it was the same: sometimes brutal and disconnected. As my perceptions changed, however, so did the medical people who worked with me! The week I was home recovering, I went to a new practitioner referred to me by a friend for cranio sacral therapy. I was hoping to find some bodywork to integrate the prosthesis and help my brain come back from anesthesia. I assumed he was a naturopathic doctor as I had heard him lecture at Bastyr University in Seattle. At the end of my session, as he was working on my left shoulder and around the implant, I started to cry. I told him that this process had allowed me to be the gentlest I had ever been with myself. It was a sweet yet heartbreaking sadness to realize that it had taken 49 years and that much trauma …but such a joy to have it arrive. I also told him this last surgery was the only time I had ever felt my past husband Chuck's presence around me. I felt him a few days before surgery and again in church the Sunday before surgery. We had been married in that Church eight years earlier on the 9th of December. The cranial-sacral practitioner asked why I thought Chuck hadn't been around. I said, without thinking, "He arrived to let me know he had never really left us." I let more tears well up and spill over. As the visit ended, the practitioner corrected my misperception that he was a naturopathic doctor. He was, in actuality, a medical doctor. He had once had a busy general practice but now enjoyed a simple but lucrative practice using hands on healing through the cranio-sacral therapy.

This completed my personal healing in regards to the medical system. It is a system with problems but has the potential for transformation to the degree that individuals within that system find their own healing and Source. These individuals are working with patients like you and me, and together we can transform the system through the alchemy of consciousness and grace. As I am able to see myself, God sees me, and, as I am able to see others, God is revealed to me.

May this story inspire you in many or small ways to become awake, including that exuberance for life! And in so doing, I hope we celebrate, honor, and cherish our

journeys together.

Chapter 12

Protocols for Breast Health

There were multiple changes I made and supplements I started during my process with breast cancer. Many I initiated from the very beginning, and others became incorporated as I learned more. I continue to learn more. I did quite a lot of research and consolidated multiple resources but tried to use what was repeated in more than one source and that had rationales that made sense to me. My goal was to eliminate the abnormal cells by boosting my immune system and to keep my other breast healthy. My mind wanted to focus on and even obsess about the supplements and protocols, but I was always reminded that my heart is the center of my healing and my mantra was and is "All is well". I regarded my emotional/spiritual experience as the most important aspect of my healing.

As George Carlin says "Life is not measured by the number of breaths we take, but by the moments that take our breath away", and I didn't want to miss any of those!

I have listed the supplements and recommended doses according to the literature and various sources that I consulted. How I followed or used these varied from where I was in the process. For example, some were used during surgery and others more during the recovery. I did vary from the recommended doses as time went on, usually decreasing doses as deficiencies were restored or as other supplements were added. As a physician, I used my knowledge, other professionals, experience, and intuition to help me choose. I would recommend consulting with a naturopathic doctor to guide you in forming your own personal protocol.

Modified Citrus Pectin and flax meal: Taking Two teaspoons daily of modified citrus pectin has been shown to inhibit metastasis in many cancers. I took this immediately following my biopsy and throughout lumpectomy/mastectomy and did continue it for several months later. I continued with flax meal 2 tablespoons /day after I discontinued the MCP. Flax helps to lower the risk of breast cancer by decreasing inflammation and by decreasing the sensitivity of cancer cells to the growth-promoting effects of estrogen. The lignan compounds found in flax protect breast cells from susceptibility to cancer initiation as well as influence insulin and growth-promoting biochemical's in the blood. There are various forms of soluble and insoluble fibers each with their own benefit. I recommend changing routines from time to time. The body likes variety, even with fibers.

Cod Liver Oil: 1-2 capsules/day of fish oil has been shown to help the immune response and to prevent metastasis. I recommend using only products that remove heavy metal contaminants and just a modest dose.

Too much oil and the cell structures that the oils are used to make may become too easily oxidized. Also, take fish oil with a meal that contains fat.

CoQ10: Up to 100mg one to three times per day is recommended. This helps with cell energy, is a powerful anti-oxidant, and also is protective with chemotherapy. I took 30-100 mg/day. This is a useful long term supplement that is powerful for heart and muscle strength and protective as an antioxidant.

Selenium: Selenium deficiency has been associated with breast cancer. Long term use of synthetic vitamin E without added selenium may cause a deficiency as it is part of the whole food vitamin E complex. Selenium works as an anti-oxidant and helps with a detoxification enzyme in the liver called glutathione peroxidase. It serves to protect the cells from DNA damage. I did 200mcg/day. Brazil nuts also high in selenium daily will provide a substantial dose. Today, I use primarily whole food vitamins so deficiencies caused by vitamin use are less likely. Whole food vitamins are complete and balanced for optimal synergistic effect.

Vitamins A, C, E, and Zinc were added prior to and post surgery though omitted several days before surgery to avoid excess bleeding. Vitamin E in the form of gamma tocopherol was added individually for some time and later changed to a whole food vitamin E. These vitamins and minerals are protective anti-oxidants against toxic chemicals, free radicals, oxidation, and stress. They promote wound healing.

Vitamin D: My levels were in a healthy range but should be tested with optimal levels of 25(OH)D around 50-70 ng/ml.

Indole-3-Carbinol was added immediately to help with the detoxification of estrogen and, thereby, deter estrogen's growth-promoting potential. This phytochemical also appears to deter the growth of breast cancer cells and moderate estrogen receptor sensitivity to estrogen. I began eating foods rich in indole-3-carbinol such as broccoli, cabbage, cauliflower, and kale. I incorporated an encapsulated assortment of those vegetables when I did not get a serving of the fresh vegetables. I was most consistent with this as it was my choice as a replacement for the recommended Tamoxafin drug. This has been shown to have many of the benefits without the side effects of the drug. My MD recommended Tamoxafin, but I chose not to take the drug. Instead, I maintained my alternative supports as best as possible. When using alternatives, one should be as fully informed as possible as to the advantages and disadvantages of both options. I encourage anyone making similar decisions to get support for informed decision-making. A decision right for me may not be the best option for someone else but do consider options.

Quercetin/Bromelain/Curcumin was added for further anti-oxidant protection. Curcumin has been shown in studies to also deter the growth of breast cancer cells. I took 2/day between meals. There are several good companies that sell these three together for theiranti-oxidative and anti-inflammatory effect.

Proteolytic Enzymes were taken after surgery to speed healing, and they are also protective for metastasis. These were between meals three times a day. Proteolytic enzymes digest and destroy protein. When taken with food, they help digest the food. When taken between meals, they will work to catalyze the destruction of protective proteins around bacteria, virus, yeast, fungi, and cancer cells.

Vitamin K was taken around surgery as I was bruising easily. Vitamin K plays an important part in blood coagulation so easy bruising may be a sign of deficiency. When vitamin K is deficient, it has been shown there is a greater susceptibility to abnormal calcifications in the aorta, bones, muscle, and breast tissue. I took 100mcg/day for several months. Up to 10mg/day is recommended.

An herbal support with milk thistle, rosemary and schiszandra was taken to help detoxify from the multiple drug exposures in surgery and recovery and also to help support estrogen metabolism.

Green Tea: I drank 4 cups/day and added 300 mg/ encapsulated green tea extract/day. The recommended dose is up to 6-8 cups/day or 500 to 700mg/day in encapsulated form. Green tea is an exceptional anti-oxidant and anti-inflammatory. It boosts the detoxification processes in the liver that protect from carcinogens. The polyphenols have been shown in some studies to inhibit the growth of breast cancer and decrease metastasis to the lungs. It also appears to lower estradiol levels that may also promote some breast cancer cells, those positive to estrogen. While on chemotherapy, green tea has also been shown to protect healthy tissue and improve the effectiveness to the cancer cells.

Avoid sugar. I was not a big sugar-eater previously but did like sweets. High insulin is known to work as a growth hormone and is increasingly being identified as a contributor to obesity and cancer. Frequent intake of refined carbohydrates, especially by themselves, can lead to frequent spikes and eventually high insulin. I focused on having some good source of protein and fat with most meals as they break down more slowly, deter the need for much insulin, and provide energy longer than a refined carbohydrate. It was difficult at times, but I found giving myself permission for a little made it easier, and I felt so

146

much more energy and vitality when the refined carbohydrates were avoided. It got easier as time went on to incorporate more nutritious foods and avoid sweets.

I began **walking** consistently 3-4 times/week. I tried to vary my exercise with the treadmill and weights to an exercise ball. As my recovery from the expansion progressed, I incorporated yoga 1-2 times/week. Exercise alone has been shown to decrease breast cancer risk, and I certainly had room to improve in this area with consistency.

I read a book on **light** just prior to being diagnosed and was impressed with the research that showed how crucial full spectrum light was for the nervous and immune system. I changed from colored to clear contact lenses, tried to get outside more often, and installed full-spectrum light bulbs in the home and office.

Body work was received fairly regularly, especially around the time of expansion. I did a series of Jin Shin Do acupressure. I found this to help so much with integrating the prosthesis and also for detoxifying from the multiple drug insults. I also had massage and cranio sacral sessions frequently for well-being and relaxation. Body work has now become a consistent part of my wellness routine.

Parabens were identified and avoided. Parabens are chemicals found in many skin products as a preservative, and they have been found in higher amounts in the breast tissue of women with breast cancer. I found a web site with products that were paraben-free and replaced my makeup and skin care with more natural and chemical-free ingredients. I ordered makeup from www.allnaturalcosmetics.com and found I loved the look and safety of using natural products. The list of potential carcinogens and endocrine disruptors in personal care products are extensive. We now use as many personal care products and household cleaning products that are free of these chemicals as possible. It is impossible to avoid them all, but whatever percentage you can do, protects you that much more! I gradually got my teenage daughter to make the change as well and realized she may be saving herself decades of exposure to potential cell damage and abnormal cell promoting chemicals.

Chlorine in water was **avoided**. I had used only filtered water at home for at least the past 15 years and in the past two years had a filter for the shower. Chlorine has been shown to be a risk factor for cancer and also to impair thyroid function. I became concerned with my daughter on a swim team but was unable to convince the pool officials about the detriment to the girls' health from the chlorine. Despite several of the girls getting chemically induced asthma attacks, the officials were unwilling to consider other forms of cleaning the water such as ozone or saline. Since I couldn't change that, I added a filter to my daughter's shower to, at least, reduce her exposure at home. Any number of filter or water treatments are out there, but any filter that eliminates chlorine is better than tap water.

My supplement regime changed as I evolved, but a supplement regime was fairly significant before, during, and after surgeries. It made sense to me that my good outcome was the result of a well thought out and researched protocol. As my knowledge evolved in relation to hormone balance, I integrated more or less products in the protocol. I have adjusted my supplement protocol over time through the use of information gained from salivary and hair analysis, kinesiology, and by the analysis of symptoms. I continue to gain increasing understanding of the interactions between the thyroid hormone, adrenal hormones, pituitary /hypothalamus hormones, and insulin. As these have become more in balance, symptoms of menopause have resolved, weight and metabolism have improved, and my immune system appears much stronger. This has become a specialty area of my practice as a Naturopath. Work with a Naturopathic Physician specializing in women's health may be recommended, but not all approach health in the same way. There are many ways to improve and restore health. Find someone that fits you and stick with it. Time with new habits is the key!

My spiritual practices and faith remains the cornerstone of my health and well-being. Practicing the Presence of God meant to me a belief in the power of Love to heal, guide, inspire, and uplift me. Practicing this as much as possible while still honoring my emotions and looking at where they came from, allowed for adjustment in my beliefs. This is such a personal journey but one I would encourage anyone with a challenge like cancer to embrace, explore, expand, and surrender to. Give up being a victim. Choose to explore and respond with as much consciousness and awareness as you can to expect and find the miracles!

Resources for more information about recommendations:

<u>Waking the Warrior Goddess Harnessing the power of Nature and Natural Medicines to</u> Achieve Extraordinary Health by Christine Horner, M.D. F.A.C.S.

<u>Doctor's Guide to Natural Medicine</u> by Dr. Paul Barney

Functional Endocrinology Lectures by Dr. Janet Lang, DC

<u>Women's Bodies, Women's Wisdom</u> by Christiane Northrup

<u>Biology of Belief</u> by Bruce Lipton

Standard Process NW, Inc.